HOPE
AT THE
BOTTOM

ADVICE FOR
—— THOSE FACING ——
FINANCIAL CHALLENGES

HOPE
AT THE
BOTTOM

VAN THURSTON
WITH MICHAEL E. TAYLOR

FOREWORD BY LARRY BURKETT

MOODY PRESS
CHICAGO

ISBN: 0-8024-1027-8

3 5 7 9 10 8 6 4

Printed in the United States of America

To Janet
my helpmate

CONTENTS

SECTION 3: LET'S TAKE ACTION

APPENDIXES

FOREWORD
by
LARRY BURKETT

Every year thousands of businesses go bankrupt in the United States. Filings for bankruptcy over the past eight years have soared by 152 percent—to well over 900,000 in both 1994 and 1995—and I expect that trend to continue.

But the stark statistics don't tell the whole story. Each bankruptcy and each case of financial distress has its own story behind it—the story of a real person or family in pain. People in bankruptcy experience shattered dreams, countless angry confrontations, bitterness, hatred and rage (toward creditors), and crushing guilt and feelings of failure. Family ties are broken. Friends often turn their backs. It isn't a pretty sight.

Without a doubt, few situations in life can strip away human dignity faster than going broke. Assets evaporate; houses are repossessed; even household furnishings are sold at auction—at a fraction of their worth. One builder I know had his truck repossessed while he was working on the roof of a house. The stories of what can happen to a person in bankruptcy defy imagination.

You may have heard the question, "Which is better—an ambulance at the bottom of the cliff or a warning sign at the top?" I suppose the appropriate answer depends on your perspective.

If you're sprawled at the bottom of the cliff, with broken bones and life-threatening injuries, you need an ambulance, complete with professionally trained EMTs who can care for you with skill and compassion.

A warning sign at the top of the cliff will not be much help at this point. It's hard to accept warnings when you're confused, in pain, and in shock. Instead, once you've recovered and are on your feet again, you can discover why you "fell," as well as how to avoid future falls.

Hope at the Bottom provides no-nonsense warnings about the horrors of bankruptcy and financial disaster, as well as caring, practical advice for those who are experiencing them. If you are considering bankruptcy, this book will serve as a sobering wake-up call.

If you are already in bankruptcy, *Hope at the Bottom* will provide invaluable, pragmatic advice on how to rebuild your life by following principles from God's Word. Most of all, the book will restore your hope.

Van Thurston has been a personal friend for many years, as well as an integral part of the Christian Financial Concepts ministry. During his career, he has personally owned twenty businesses. Under Van's direction, CFC developed the "Business by the Book" seminar, which has ministered to thousands over the last decade. He knows what comprises good business practice.

Van now serves as the president of Turnaround Ministries, through which he ministers to thousands of couples in financial distress. God has given him the ability to listen compassionately to those who are hurting, along with the ability to firmly speak the truth to them.

Van Thurston and Mike Taylor have worked together to produce *Hope at the Bottom,* a great resource that we trust God will use in a mighty way to bring healing and hope to those who need it the most. If you are among the thousands in America who are on the edge of the cliff of financial disaster, read this book. We pray that, through it, God will supply what you need to get on your feet again financially and back on track with His plan for your life.

LARRY BURKETT

Now to Him who is able to do exceeding abundantly beyond all that we ask or think, according to the power that works within us, to Him be the glory in the church and in Christ Jesus to all generations forever and ever. Amen.
(Ephesians 3:20–21)

SECTION ONE

LAYING THE FOUNDATION

CHAPTER 1
THERE IS
A WAY OUT

Are you in deep financial trouble with nowhere to turn? Are you depressed, feeling alone and rejected? Have you thought of suicide? Have you and your mate stopped talking? Have you considered bankruptcy or even filed for it? Do you see no way out of your problems?

If you answered yes to any of the above questions, *I have great news for you:* There is a way out of your problems. I know. I've been where you are. I know what you are feeling. But I got out, and I know a lot of others who have too. If I can get out, anyone can.

I learned the hard way. I found hope at the bottom by being a slow learner, not an expert. The only reason I didn't make more mistakes was that I didn't think of them. So keep reading, because you'll learn how to take the pressure off and regain hope in your life. And I mean now—not next month or next year.

Here is a true story about someone who, like me and maybe like you, made some dumb mistakes (names and details have been changed). Bill was angry when he phoned me. He said that all he needed was a little more time. If the bank would just give him until the following

Monday morning! But time had run out; his construction company would have to fold. There was no way out. After all, even a strong man can tread water only so long.

The longer Bill talked the more I realized how serious the problem was. He had *forged his wife's name to personally guarantee the bank loans,* and as a result, he was going to lose everything he and his wife had worked for over the last twelve years. *Everything.* The house, the cars, the club. It was hard for me to keep Bill focused on telling me the details. He was so overcome with guilt, fear, and anger. He had seen others go bankrupt before, and it had been brutal. All his mistakes had caught up to him, and he knew it. The running was over.

And what about his mother and father? At Bill's request (and over his brother's objections) his parents had loaned Bill their life savings to help start his construction company. He assured them that their money was safe, that he wouldn't do anything risky, and that there was nothing to worry about. Now he would have to face them and explain how he lost all their money.

I could feel Bill's pain over the phone. He kept saying, "It's all my fault; it's all my fault." Bill had failed his wife, Doris, his children, and his parents. When the bank sold the homes he had built, they held Bill responsible for the outstanding balances on his loans. He lost everything of the slightest value in order to pay the debts.

In Bill's eyes, he was a miserable failure to everyone, including God. He no longer had much to live for. The rejection he felt from others only drove him more deeply into a depression with no apparent way out. He said to me, "I'm hurting. I didn't mean to hurt anyone. I thought I was doing what was best, but I was wrong. What do I do now?"

He was at the bottom of the barrel with only one way to look—up. And he did look up.

THE SOURCE OF BILL'S HOPE

Bill followed the principles outlined in this book, and, before long, he had the peace and joy we all search for. You can have the same peace and joy. You don't have to be miserable. There is a way out.

Bill and his wife are rebuilding their marriage with an open and transparent relationship, but it is going to take some time. It was not damaged in a day and it will not be restored in a day. He's still in the construction business but on a much, much smaller scale. Without borrowing any additional money or signing a guarantee, he has been able to support his family with a modest lifestyle and start paying back his suppliers and the bank. It will take him several more years to pay off his creditors, but all of them, except one, are working with him. Bill takes time for his family now—quality time. He also takes time to help other businesspeople avoid the mistakes he made.

I know that sounds almost too easy. It was not then and is not now. Bill has had sleepless nights and lonesome days in his struggle to rebuild his life using God's principles. It's tough. There is no shortcut. But there is a way out.

I remember Walt Meloon, whose story is told in *On the Waters of the World*, showing me the Bible he used when the Meloon family was going through the bankruptcy of the family business, Correct Craft Boats. His anchor verse was Proverbs 3:5–6. You could hardly read that portion of his Bible because of the tears he shed over years of struggling, praying, and seeking God's direction.

Bill will probably live in a rented duplex and drive a borrowed pickup for several years. He still owes a lot of money, but he has found, in his own words, "a peace and a joy that I have always been looking for."

. If that's what you want, you can have it. I have seen scores of people with similar success stories. Do you want to be one of them?

BANKRUPTCY CAN
VICTIMIZE WOMEN TOO

Bankruptcy is an equal opportunity horror that plagues men and women alike. According to Dun and Bradstreet, the number of businesses owned by women in the United States jumped 18 percent from 1991 to 1994, and their businesses now employ more workers than Fortune 500 companies do *globally*. According to the Census Bureau women own one-third of all U.S. businesses and a staggering 40 percent of retail and service businesses.[1] That is why I am getting almost as many calls from women as men about problems in their businesses. One of the nice things about counseling with women business owners is that most are ready to deal with the problem.

Through a combination of circumstances, Susan found herself in bankruptcy. Her father built his career in the construction business, and she literally spent most of her childhood in his office. As she got older, her dad entrusted more and more responsibility to her, and she learned the construction business thoroughly. When Susan married and started a family of her own, however, she left the day-to-day operations.

Then her father died suddenly. Because her mother was not well and knew nothing about running the business, Susan stepped in to help. For the first two years, things ran smoothly. Then came the recession of the early 1990s, and work dried up in her region of the country. Cash flow tightened. Because she was a little unsure of whom to lay off, Susan kept her employees too long, and the business began to lose money. She got behind with her creditors, and when things worsened more, the bank called her loan. She defaulted, and bankruptcy proceedings began.

Susan's husband, Ralph, encouraged her all along, and he helped her to carry the emotional burden. He knew how much her dad's business meant to Susan. After much prayer and talking with bank officials, the two were granted an extension of time. The bankruptcy process was halted. The company was reduced to four employees, and it began to do a modest amount of building and repair work in spite of the recession.

This story has a happy ending. After nearly five years, Susan made the last payment to her bank. And since the business was consistently showing a profit again, she was able to sell it, realizing that she wanted to be at home with her children, running her household instead of a business.

The point is, financial difficulties and bankruptcy show no gender partiality.

IT CAN HAPPEN FOR YOU

If God will do it for Bill and Susan, if He has done it for me, He will do it for you as well. You can be at peace when you lie down at night. I'm not talking about cheap gimmicks or fly-by-night motivational programs. I mean the real thing, real hope. I'm talking about seeing a change *now*. I mean being glad to get up in the morning and face the day.

You may have a hard time believing all this. Hope that things can turn around for you may be a little slim right now. But if you're thin on hope, borrow some from me. I have hope—plenty of it. I believe in you even when you don't believe in yourself. Listen to me and I will show you how to regain hope and direction for your life.

If you're like the rest of us, you tried it your way and it hasn't worked. You've done everything you could to correct, improve, and change, only to see everything slipping away, leaving you with nothing. You may have lost your job, your family, and your home. It does not matter where you are or what your circumstances are. What matters is whether or not you are ready to deal with the real issues in your life and do something about them.

Jesus said, "These things I have spoken to you, so that in Me you may have peace. In the world you have tribulation, but take courage; I have overcome the world" (John 16:33). God wants to pull you out of the mess you're in. You literally have His Word: "And we know that God causes all things to work together for good to those who love God, to those who are called according to His purpose" (Romans 8:28).

I've been where you are and back, and I want to help you get your life together. God is pulling for you, and so am I. I know that the life-changing principles in this book work because they worked for me and hundreds of others just like Bill and Susan. These principles have changed their lives and brought the peace and joy they needed. These principles can work for you, but you must decide to join the team. You must have an open and teachable spirit. You must be willing to listen.

HERE'S A WAY OUT THAT WORKS

God's means of deliverance for you seldom includes a magic wand that eliminates all your problems. That would be nice, but it's not His style. His plan is to work *with* you and *through* you. Like a good football coach, He'll call the plays, but you need to run with the ball. He'll show you how, but you have to do the legwork.

If your life is in enough turmoil right now, you'll really want change. If you're not ready for change, however, maybe your life hasn't become complicated enough. Maybe the fire is not hot enough. That's not being mean-spirited. I just know that most people who are hurting want relief at any price. Pain makes a person ready to do business with God. Are you open to change? I've always been closer to God when I was in the valley. Despair and difficulty produce a very teachable spirit in me. What about you?

Things may be mixed up right now, but so what? Did you really expect life to be smooth sailing every day, every year? If you're like the rest of us, when things get this bad, we get down and depressed. Things can cave in on us in a heartbeat, and we can't see a way out.

Your problems will get more complicated when you seek relief in the wrong ways—resentment, blaming others (even hating them), divorce, suicide, drinking, bitterness, cheating on your spouse, stealing, lying. Those behaviors don't work, and that may be why you're reading this book.

It really is possible to be successful and to have peace and joy in your life. And I mean more than just "not being broke." I mean really being happy, content, and at peace with everyone. You can face your creditors, the sheriff, your friends, your family, and even the IRS without feeling shame or fear. You can sleep well at night without the fear of waking up the next morning.

Isn't that what you want? If it is, I'm going to teach you how you can turn your life around. Unless you have a better plan, you don't have anything to lose. And I suspect you might be sick and tired of creating your own plans by now.

This is your book now. Mark it up, underline in it, do whatever you need to get the most from it. Consider it your manual for victory.

PERSONAL COMMITMENT: This is the date that I made a commitment to read this book from cover to cover:

_____   _____

YOUR SIGNATURE   DATE

CONCLUDING PRINCIPLE:

> *You must want to change in order to change.*

---

1. "Women in Business," *USA Today*, 12 April 1995, C-1.

CHAPTER 2
IT'S NOT FAIR

I remember a time in my life when everything seemed to go wrong: The bank called my loan, I couldn't get any more credit from my suppliers, my best employee went to work for my competitor, people who owed me money would not pay me, and the people I owed demanded payment and threatened to sue me. My children were sick, my wife was in the hospital, our home burned, the car broke down, the phone rang without stopping, the dog got run over, and I broke a tooth.

I know what it's like when life is unfair, and I've counseled with hundreds of hurting men and women in business who have had equally bad, or worse, things happen to them. So I have a good idea what you may be going through right now and how you are feeling.

ARE YOU STRESSED TO
THE POINT OF BREAKING?

The following exercise might help you understand some of the things you're dealing with, perhaps on a day-to-day basis. Put a checkmark by each item that expresses how you feel or what might be going on in your life. When you finish, add up the checkmarks. You might be surprised at just how much stress and chaos you have right now. You may be doing a lot bet-

ter than you think, considering the heavy load you are
bearing.

☐ In trouble	☐ Embarrassed
☐ Broke or close to it	☐ Depressed
☐ In trouble with the IRS	☐ Can't sleep
☐ Scared	☐ Ashamed
☐ Have overwhelming fear	☐ Guilty
☐ Have panic attacks	☐ Lonely
☐ Unable to pray at times	☐ Rejected
☐ Feel God is not with you	☐ Isolated
☐ Ask God, "Why?"	☐ Don't know what to do
☐ Feel punished by God	☐ God does not hear you
☐ Hatred for those who caused the problem:	☐ Feel abandoned by God
☐ the court	☐ Cut off
☐ lawyers	☐ No hope
☐ bad employees	☐ No future
☐ IRS	☐ Thoughts of suicide
☐ husband or wife	☐ Considering/already divorced
☐ Feeling like a failure to:	☐ Thoughts of running away
☐ yourself	☐ Can't take anymore
☐ family	☐ Feel bad/tired all the time
☐ God	☐ Sick a lot
☐ Things are out of control	☐ Denial
☐ Problems with spouse	☐ Asking God to take you home
☐ Problems with children	☐ Pressure is too much
☐ Unmanageable stress level	☐ Angry
☐ Creditors harassing you all the time	

Total items checked: _____

Even if you checked only one, that's too many. But that's the way life is. Without conflict we would never grow.

If you're upset because you believe that what you're going through is not fair, being upset won't help, although it's normal to be upset or depressed. From your viewpoint, you can't see that you have done anything to deserve this. But lashing out won't help either. And it may appear that others never have it this bad, but that is not always true.

There's a danger in dwelling on whether something is fair or not: You will start having a pity party. You will stop thinking of ways to solve your problems, spending more time instead on blaming someone else.

THE BIBLE AND FAIRNESS

The fact is, life isn't fair. Being treated unfairly puts you in the elite company of biblical heroes such as Joseph, Moses, David, Paul, and even Jesus Christ. God tells us that most of His saints went through some extremely tough times before He could use them.

Remember Joseph? Was life fair to him? He was thrown into a well by his brothers, sold into slavery, and locked up in prison. When he got out, he ended up being returned to prison—and he didn't do anything wrong! Think of Moses and Job. Did they get a fair shake in life? How about Paul? He was beaten with rods three times, stoned once, shipwrecked three times, and spent a night and a day in the open sea. He was the Lord's "main man" to the Gentiles. Did he deserve that treatment? What about Jesus? He lived a perfect life, bringing healing, hope, and mercy to so many. He was killed by those He was trying to save.

In more recent times, Ralph and Walt Meloon, owners of Correct Craft Boats, were forced into bankruptcy in 1958 specifically because they chose to be obedient to Jesus in their business. They did the right thing. They honored God. And then, boom! For doing what was right, they were forced into bankruptcy. Just because it didn't seem fair did not relieve them of their responsibilities. They still had to continue doing what was right in the sight of God. It took them twenty-six years to pay off their debts even though a human court said they did not owe them.

Think of Larry Burkett, president and founder of Christian Financial Concepts, a ministry that has helped thousands of Christians get their lives in order. Larry has had a heart attack and two operations for cancer.

Don't you know that God had your best interest in mind when He gave you Philippians 4:8? "Finally, brethren, whatever is true, whatever is honorable, whatever is right, whatever is pure, whatever is lovely, whatever is of good repute, if there is any excellence and if anything worthy of praise, let your mind dwell on these things." God put that verse in the Bible for your good, to help you have victory and to overcome adverse circumstances. God loves you, and He wants you to have an abundant life.

GUESS WHO I MET AT THE BOTTOM

I can remember very clearly when everything had gone wrong for me. All I wanted was out of my problems. I didn't want any lessons, molding, or shaping. I was hurting—I wanted relief, and I wanted it right then. But God knew what was best for me. He loved me so much that He allowed me to get to the bottom—all the way to the bottom.

At first I thought that my problems had to be someone else's fault. But when I accepted responsibility for where I was and stopped blaming God, my fellowship with God became real. I knew who He was. I understood that the bottom was the best place I had ever been. That probably sounds crazy, but you may say those same words one day. At the bottom I really began to know God. You don't necessarily have to go to the bottom to have a close personal relationship with God, but for hard heads like me it seems the only way.

When you're hurting enough, you can talk to God from the standpoint of needs, not wants. You can get rid of all the worldly things in your prayers. You get serious when there is nothing conditional in your prayers, no bargaining.

LIFE AFTER UNFAIR TREATMENT

Fairness is not the issue—let's get that settled. Life is not fair. When people tell me that they haven't been treated fairly, I believe them, but neither am I surprised. The question is, How are you going to live after being treated unfairly? Are you going to strike back? Are you going to simmer in bitterness? Will you be consumed by this?

The greatest Christian people I have ever known have had tremendous unfairness in their lives, but they managed to put it behind them. They got on with their lives. As long as your focus in life is to convince everybody that you've been treated unfairly, you'll miss out. Most people already know that life isn't fair. Welcome to the club. You cannot let the thoughts of what has happened stop you from getting on with your life. Thoughts of unfairness will stop you from solving your problems. You can spend one minute, one hour, one day, or the rest of your life bogged down with this unfairness issue. Or you can choose to put it behind you. I challenge you to put it down and get rid of it.

PERSONAL COMMITMENT: I have dealt with thinking about and dwelling on unfairness in my life on the date below. With God's grace and strength, I choose to get on with my life and to consider it all joy. "Consider it all joy, my brethren, when you encounter various trials" (James 1:2).

_____   _____

YOUR SIGNATURE   DATE

CONCLUDING PRINCIPLE:

> *Life is unfair. So what?*

CHAPTER 3
LONG-TERM SOLUTIONS

I know that you need help right now. I know that you are having very difficult times. I understand that you need a solution to your problems. But quick fixes seldom exist. In a year, or maybe even less, you could be back in the same situation. You could even be in worse shape.

Suppose we tried to solve one issue in your life—money, for instance. The real problem could be something else. Money problems are usually a symptom rather than the actual problem. I have often found the real problem to be attitude.

I want you to have all the things that God wants you to have, including an abundant life of peace and joy. But you have to look at it as a long-term, permanent solution that will equip you to handle difficulties and problems. You and I both know that, if you had every problem solved, $10 million in the bank, a perfect marriage (if married), perfect children, a perfect home, a perfect business, and a perfect job, by six o'clock in the morning something would go wrong. You need to be equipped so that the good things don't become a problem but rather an opportunity.

Long-term, solid solutions will allow you to accomplish the things in life that you want to. I think of the times when I have been in pain or when I was sick. I didn't want anybody to give me all the reasons I was sick. I didn't want them to explain the theory of what would make me well. I wanted the pain to stop. I wanted to feel better! If you have ever had a kidney stone, you know the only thing you want is relief. That's what it is like when you are in a painful financial condition. You need some relief. True relief comes from long-term solutions.

WHY SHORT-TERM
SOLUTIONS DON'T WORK

Short-term solutions postpone dealing with the real issues. For instance, several years ago the president of a company phoned and said that he had a severe cash flow problem. Even though the business was an incredible money-maker, it was simply out of money. The president explained that some investors who had verbally committed to supply operating funds had backed out on him. I told him about factoring and suggested that he go to his bank to see if they had a factoring department. When he was able to secure the money he needed by factoring the business accounts, I thought the problem was solved.

About a year later, I heard that the company had closed its doors and that the rest of the investors had lost more than $500,000. I was disturbed to discover that the failure of the company had been caused by the immorality of the president, a very active Christian. His customers' growing awareness of his immorality took away his credibility, and, in his particular type of business, credibility was everything.

The president chose a short-term solution—more money—rather than the long-term solution of getting his life under the lordship of Jesus Christ. A short-term solution may only patch up or postpone dealing with your *real* problems.

Now, you may not be involved in immorality or anything illegal. But you may be so distracted by seeking short-term solutions that you miss the real issues that require longer-term efforts. It could be that you need to deal with problems in your marriage. Or maybe you have some sin that has not been dealt with. Perhaps you should not be in business at all. The challenge is to avoid the temptation of short-term solutions and get to the real issues of your life and work.

SELDOM IS MORE MONEY THE ANSWER

Most of the problems people have are caused by themselves. When looked at from a short-term viewpoint, it is easy to conclude that the solution to not having enough money is to get more. That's not always true.

I have heard Larry Burkett say that many people he has counseled already knew the solution to their problem—or so they thought. One said, "I'm making $30,000 a year. All I need is $10,000 more to solve all my problems." The very next day another person, who was making $40,000 a year, came in and said, "All I need is $20,000 more to solve my problems." Later that day a lawyer came in and said, "I make $100,000 a year, and, if I could get $25,000 more, I could solve my problems." The next day an open-heart surgeon came in and said that all he needed was a couple hundred thousand dollars, and he could solve his problems. Without exception, each person thought the solution was as simple as more money.

The reason these people were having problems was too much spending, not too little income. They were not good stewards of what they already had. Some who talked to Larry got on a budget and got their finances straightened out. They dealt with their spending patterns and, as a result, arrived at a long-term solution. Some are making half of what they were making and living better. The solution to their problems was not more money.

COMPLEX PROBLEMS DEMAND LONG-TERM ANSWERS

I want you to rethink what your ideal life would be like. Not just for tomorrow, but for the rest of your life. To get beyond present problems—and stay out of them in the future—it is necessary to master thinking long term when you work on your solution. I am not saying that you don't need to pay your rent or utility bill or that you might be put out on the street. I know you need today's basic necessities. But money is not the ultimate answer in life.

I have known people worth $10 million who have committed suicide. I know people who have lost millions of dollars and today are broke. They don't want their money back. They have a closer relationship with Jesus Christ than they ever had when they were wealthy.

You need to rethink what your long-term goals are. Would you like to have a good, warm, personal, close relationship with Jesus Christ and know that you are in the center of His will? When you lay your head down at night, can you praise Him and thank Him for the day?

If you are married, does your spouse really honor and respect you? Does he or she love you? Do you have a good relationship—one where you share openly and where you can't wait to see each other? Are you excited to see him or her?

If you have children, do you have a good relationship with them? It doesn't matter if they're still young or if they are adults. Do you have the kind of relationship that you are glad to see each other, that you encourage each other and share with each other? Are you telling your children some of the mistakes you have made so that they won't make them? Are they listening to you? Have you allowed that kind of communication to develop?

Are you helping other people? Are you reflecting Jesus Christ on the job and to your neighbors? Do you have your act together?

When you think, *What would I really like to have and be like?* what do you think about? I am not talking about possessions or money—$1 million or $10 million. I am talking about rethinking the quality of your life. The quality of your life is not based on possessions or what position you have attained, whether you are president of a corporation or own a company. Rather, success and happiness are based on your relationship with God and those around you.

Being able to put my arms around my children, who are now adults with children of their own, and tell them how much I love them and hear them say, "I love you," even when it's in the middle of an airport—that's success. To hear one of my grandsons praying and saying, "Thank you, God, for letting us be at 'Na-Na' and 'Ga-Ga's' house," and then kissing me good night—

that's living. No matter how much money there is, there's not enough to take the place of that kind of relationship.

So you need to take some time to think through long-term solutions for your problems. Once Dr. Dobson related over the radio a conversation he had with his father. He asked his father what he would like on his tombstone when he died. His father replied in two words: "He prayed." He had a long-term viewpoint.

PERSONAL COMMITMENT: "Lord, I come to You now and ask that You put in my heart a desire for a long-term solution to my problems, not a quick fix. I want to get my life straightened out. Help me to understand what Your solution is, not mine or the world's. And help me to do what You tell me to do."

When you have finished praying that prayer, sign your name below and date it.

_____   _____
YOUR SIGNATURE   DATE

CONCLUDING PRINCIPLE:

*Finish the race
to win the prize.*

CHAPTER 4

BE SURE WHERE YOUR LADDER IS LEANING

Have you ever, without a doubt, had the right answer to a question, problem, market, loan, disagreement, or whatever, and then discovered that you didn't ask the right question? I have. Hundreds of times.

I have never gone to my wife or banker or anybody else with an idea and said, "Let me show you this great idea that I have on how I can lose money—I want to tell you all the details. It's great. I can hardly wait to start."

I go to my wife all the time with my bright, new ideas. She'll say something like, "I have a funny feeling about that," or, "I don't think you should hire that person," or some other comment. My answer to her reservations used to be, "Are you sick? What do you mean, 'funny feeling'? Give me some cold, hard facts for what you're saying or I'm going ahead." I had the right answers; the problem was I had the wrong questions.

That's precisely what John did. He had reached the

top, the apex of his career, and had a net worth of more than $20 million. Yet on his deathbed he told his wife and attorney, "What difference does it all make? I have all this money, power, fame, and now it means nothing. Is this all there is in life?"

Now that's despair. That's the confession of a brokenhearted man who chased success all his life, only to discover on his deathbed that he was really chasing an illusion. His right answer was, "If you get enough, you will have peace, joy, and contentment someday." He got the right answer to what he was seeking. But John asked the wrong question. Do you?

What are you living your life for? I have often heard Ted DeMoss, president of the Christian Businessmen's Committee, say that climbing the ladder of success is immaterial if the ladder is leaning against the wrong building. You may get to the top only to find that's not where you wanted to be. What if you work your whole lifetime, fighting, clawing, scratching to reach the top of your career ladder, only to learn it's been propped against the wrong building? By that time, it's too late to switch ladders. *Don't let that happen to you!*

I'll never forget the blunder I made in my engineering drawing class in college. The professor's assignment was to reproduce the drawings from section eight of the textbook. I must have been daydreaming when the assignment was given because I did all the drawings from *section nine*. For two weeks I meticulously labored over those drawings. I agonized over each detail. Every line was crisp. There wasn't a single smudge. The drawings were perfect.

On the due date, I turned them in with great pride

and satisfaction, only to hear the professor say, "Those are great drawings. They're just the wrong ones. The assignment was from section eight."

I got a zero for my work. *I had the right answers but the wrong assignment!*

I've worked with hundreds of people in financial distress, and I can tell you that many good, kind, smart, and self-confident people *think* they have all the right answers. But unless they are in a right relationship with God, they are answering the wrong questions. Jesus said it best in Mark 8:36: "What does it profit a man to gain the whole world, and forfeit his soul?"

Are you are dealing with the right questions in life—*real questions that matter*—such as, What's going to happen when I die? Is more better? Is this all there is in life? Don't be like the man named John. Trying to get all the "things" you can may satisfy for a while, but not in the long run.

When you construct a building that you expect to endure, you start with a good foundation. The taller the building, the deeper and more solid the foundation. As you read this chapter, be sure that you have laid the right foundation for your life.

Take time to read this material slowly. Everything you read in this book will be a waste of time without getting this part right. Getting the right foundation for your life is the most important thing you will ever do.

Don't pass over this by saying, "This doesn't apply to me." If you say you're going to heaven, do you know why? And does your reason agree with what the Bible says? Let's settle the issue of eternal salvation now. It's the most important issue of your entire life. If you haven't come to grips with your salvation, your ladder is leaning against the wrong wall. And the day will come when you'll regret it.

You may be one of those precious people who started acting like a Christian, doing the right things, saying the right things, and rarely doing anything wrong. You may read your Bible, have a quiet time, maybe even teach Sunday school. You might have walked down the aisle and been immersed or sprinkled or whatever. Your parents may have been missionaries or just plain good folks. But if you've never repented of your sins and accepted Jesus Christ as Lord and Savior, the Bible says you're not a Christian, meaning you're not saved.

Maybe you're just not sure that you're going to heaven. In your heart of hearts, you're not positive. God understands, but He wants you to know with full confidence that you're saved. You need to be sure. You need to know and have this issue settled. It's the true foundation for your whole life.

I said I would give you information that would lead you out of the bottom of the barrel. Here it is. Follow the steps below to accept Jesus Christ as your personal Lord and Savior and to obtain a complete assurance that you're heaven-bound.

FOUNDATION FOR SUCCESS—
Become a Christian

1. *Recognize* that you don't become a Christian because you are good or because you refrain from doing bad things. God's Word says, "There is none who does good, there is not even one" (Romans 3:12). Maybe you've never murdered,

stolen, or committed adultery. That's great. But you're still not saved unless you have a Savior in Jesus Christ.

2. *Recognize* that you are not necessarily a Christian because you are a member of some church, for again God's Word declares that many are "holding to a form of godliness, although they have denied its power" (2 Timothy 3:5).

3. *Confess* that you are a guilty sinner in God's sight, for you have broken His commandments. Indeed, all the world has become guilty before Him (Romans 3:19).

4. *Confess* that you cannot save yourself, for "by grace you have been saved through faith; and that not of yourselves, it is the gift of God" (Ephesians 2:8).

5. *Confess* that you are hopelessly lost and under condemnation without Jesus Christ as your personal Savior, for He said, "The Son of Man has come to seek and to save that which was lost" (Luke 19:10).

6. *Believe* the good news that Christ died for the ungodly (Romans 5:8). He therefore died for you and settled your sin debt on Calvary's cross.

7. *Believe* the glorious news that Christ was raised from the dead and, by the power of God, is now able to save all who come to God through Him (Hebrews 7:25).

8. *Call* on the name of the Lord Jesus in prayer with
    a sincere desire to be saved from your sins, for
    God has promised that "whoever will call upon
    the name of the Lord will be saved" (Romans
    10:13; see also Joel 2:32; Acts 2:21).

9. *Rely* on God's sure promise, not on your feelings,
    and by faith declare that you are saved by the
    blood of Jesus Christ, shed for the forgiveness of
    your sins, and openly confess Him as your Savior
    and Lord (Romans 10:9–10).

PERSONAL COMMITMENT: On this date I repented of my
sins and asked Jesus Christ to come into my heart to
take control of my life.

_____   _____

YOUR SIGNATURE   DATE

*I shared this most important event in my life with the fol-
lowing people:*

_____   _____

_____   _____

_____   _____

_____   _____

CONCLUDING PRINCIPLE:

> *The foundation for true success is being in a right relationship with God through faith in Jesus Christ.*

CHAPTER 5
KEEP YOUR ACT TOGETHER

What if I told you that I had recently discovered a book that is used by the most successful people in the world and that you can get a copy? This book will not only show you how to deal with all future problems but also how you can have peace, joy, and success in spite of your problems. It will show you how you can have the happiest spouse in the world, how to be content, and how to prosper. The list goes on and on, but I'm sure you get the idea.

How much would you give for a copy? What have you paid for training, seminars, or counseling? It doesn't take long to spend a lot of money in those areas. If you had such a book, how much time and effort would you put into studying the book and doing what it told you to do? I don't know about you, but I would spend every spare minute I had. How often would you study it? Would you call up the author? Would you take his advice? If you had access to this book, would you search it to learn about joy, success, and peace?

I am speaking, of course, of the Bible. It is nothing less than the guidebook for success in life.

Maybe you have tried to live for Christ in the past,

but you have grown tired of the up-and-down, hot-and-cold, roller-coaster experience with Him. "It doesn't work," you say. I agree that an on-again, off-again relationship with Jesus doesn't work, but have you faithfully studied God's instruction book to learn how to do it right?

I have found that if I miss one day reading God's Word, meditating on what it says, and praying, I start drifting. I lose a sense for what's right and wrong. I have wrong thoughts. I start getting a bad attitude. I start doing things Jesus would not want me to do, knowing all the time they are dead wrong. I know I'm going to get burned, and I do it anyway. Isn't that dumb?

My life gets out of balance without daily correction from God's Word. What about you? Once you get your act together by accepting Jesus Christ as your personal Savior, you have to *keep your act together* by staying in the Word—every day. Not every other day, or when you don't have anything else to do, or when you can make time—every day. Committing yourself to doing certain things will help you grow in a vibrant, life-changing relationship with the Lord Jesus Christ.

1. SCHEDULE A SPECIFIC PLACE AND TIME TO READ THE BIBLE DAILY

There is no better way to learn how God wants you to live than to read the Instruction Book of life every day. Do you read the newspaper every day? Do you read the mail? As a creature of habit, you likely do so at the same place or time each day. Likewise, you'll be more consistent in your Bible reading if you plan to read at the same time every day.

How can you possibly know what to do, especially

if you're in trouble, unless you read the Guidebook every day? Read how Luke describes the Christians who lived in Berea and consider if you could be described in the same way: "Now these were more noble-minded than those in Thessalonica, for they received the word with great eagerness, examining the Scriptures daily, to see whether these things were so" (Acts 17:11).

Beware of this: Some days you will feel like you're getting nowhere reading the Bible. Keep on. God hasn't lost sight of you. The Word will never let you down. Rome wasn't built in a day, and neither will God rebuild your life in a day. A beautiful building is constructed carefully and precisely, following directions one day at a time.

2. Obey God

What is the point in finding the best way to live if you don't live by it? If you're really grateful for what God has done for you, then obey what God says. It's that simple: "He who has My commandments and keeps them is the one who loves Me; and he who loves Me will be loved by My Father, and I will love him and will disclose Myself to him" (John 14:21).

That's not hard to understand. Obey Him, and He will disclose more of Himself to you. Ignore or disobey Him, and you will not be able to see Him clearly. And you know the confusion that can result from that, don't you?

3. Pray Daily

Simply talk to God, and listen when He talks back to you. This is a vital part of being in a relationship with

anyone: You must take time to talk and listen to one
another. You don't have to use a lot of fancy words. Just
talk to Him like you would a close friend. Prayer is like
a child talking to his father. It can be about anything:

- crying out for help
- sharing hurts and loneliness
- feeling scared
- being depressed
- feeling excited and happy
- praise for who God is or answered prayers
- just telling God that you love Him

Maybe a typical prayer for you would go something like this: "Oh, God, I really messed up this morning with my wife. I was wrong when I lost my temper
with her. Will You forgive me and give me what it takes
to ask for her forgiveness?"

God wants you to come to Him for everything. The
key to having your prayers answered is abiding in
Jesus. Here's exactly what Jesus said: "If you abide in
Me, and My words abide in you, ask whatever you
wish, and it will be done for you" (John 15:7).

You may think He doesn't hear, but He does. He
wants to give you the desires of your heart, but often
He has something much better than what you ask. So if
His answer to your prayer is no, don't give up. Watch
for something better.

4. WITNESS FOR CHRIST

I'm not necessarily talking about preaching in a
church or standing on a street corner telling people
about Jesus. That may be what God calls you to do, but

maybe not. What He does call us to do is to live in a way that shows we are Christians. That means letting Jesus live in us every day so that people can see Him in our actions and words.

That doesn't mean that you walk around all day talking about Jesus. But it does mean that you remain connected to Jesus—you "abide" in Him.

5. Trust God with the Details

Once you have come under the lordship of Jesus Christ, trust Him with all the details of your life, not just the "big" decisions, for He is faithful in even the little ones: "Commit your way to the Lord, trust also in Him, and He will do it" (Psalm 37:5). You may think that God couldn't possibly be interested in the tiny little details you face every day, but He is.

Don't believe for one minute that God is unable to handle the details of your life. Remember, He created everything, He knows the end from the beginning, He is the Alpha and Omega, and He allowed His Son to die for your sins. God paid a heavy price to have you in heaven with Him. So of course He is trustworthy enough to hear your prayers and answer them.

He *is* trustworthy. He *does* hear. And He *will* answer you!

6. Allow the Holy Spirit to Fill Your Life

It is the Holy Spirit who makes Jesus Christ real in us. Jesus sent the Holy Spirit to His disciples when He went away to be with His Father:

> And I will ask the Father, and He will give you another Helper, that He may be with you forever; that is the

Spirit of truth, whom the world cannot receive, because it does not see Him or know Him, but you know Him because He abides with you and will be in you. I will not leave you as orphans; I will come to you. (John 14:16–18)

As gasoline is to an automobile engine, so the Holy Spirit is to you as a believer. Without Him and His power you're going nowhere. He gives *supernatural power,* exactly what it takes to live the life God wants you to live. In other words, *God not only calls you to holiness, He also supplies the power for you to be holy:* "But you will receive power when the Holy Spirit has come upon you; and you shall be My witnesses both in Jerusalem, and in all Judea and Samaria, and even to the remotest part of the earth" (Acts 1:8). What a wonderful God we serve!

With the Holy Spirit filling your life, you will begin to experience the life of Jesus Christ in you. You will begin to see love, joy, peace, patience, kindness, goodness, faithfulness, gentleness, and self-control. Although this won't happen overnight, as though you flipped a light switch, you will begin to notice a difference. So will others. The change will be slow at first, but things will change as fast as you can handle them. Be filled with the Spirit, and then *fasten your seat belt!*

PERSONAL COMMITMENT: Today I made a commitment to the Lord to spend part of each day with Him—talking to Him, listening to Him, reading His Word, and meditating on how He wants me to live for Him.

_____   _____

YOUR SIGNATURE   DATE

I told the following people about this commitment:

_____   _____

_____   _____

CONCLUDING PRINCIPLE:

> ### *Without daily reading of the Instruction Book, you can't have true wisdom.*

CHAPTER 6

PRAISE GOD FOR YOUR CIRCUMSTANCES

You and I typically tend to do one of three things when life gets tough for a time: We grow bitter toward God, ignore God altogether, or learn to praise God in our circumstances. Which category most frequently describes you? Choices one and two will only make matters worse, since ultimately God alone can show you how to straighten out your problems. After all, if your car needs repairs, you take it to someone who knows how to repair it. When your life needs to be repaired, you need your Maker's counsel.

How and why should you praise God for whatever difficulties you're facing? Bleak as things may be, you have to acknowledge that God is in control of your life. If you don't, you close down the communication lines with Him, and that's not a good move. Don't alienate yourself from the One who made you! Contemplate the following reasons for praising God in spite of your circumstances.

THE NATURE OF PRAISE

1. PRAISE CONFIRMS GOD'S PRESENCE IN YOUR LIFE AND THAT HE'S "IN CONTROL"

You may not feel like He's in control. In fact, you may feel like He has let things get out of control and does not even know you exist. King David felt that way sometimes, and here is his response:

> My God, my God, why have You forsaken me? Far from my deliverance are the words of my groaning. O my God, I cry by day, but You do not answer; and by night, but I have no rest. Yet You are holy, O You *who are enthroned upon the praises of Israel*. (Psalm 22:1–3, italics added)

Even in his agony, King David realized that God is *enthroned upon the praise of His people!* That means that wherever God is praised He is present. When you praise God, you *confirm* His presence in and control over you. But beyond simply being with you, He is your *advocate*. God is working for the very best in your life.

When you praise God, you not only confirm that God is with you, but that He is also putting divine power to work in your situation. Even though you've made mistakes, He's still on your side. John 1:14 states that Jesus Christ is "full of grace and truth." Grace simply means that He chooses to continue loving you and to be your advocate even though you don't deserve it. That kind of love, grace, and forgiveness is difficult for the human imagination to fathom, but it's true. You can see how that kind of divine character solicits praise.

2. PRAISE GETS YOUR ATTENTION OFF YOURSELF AND ONTO GOD

When problems become oppressive and it seems like every human being on earth is angry with you, it's easy to lose perspective. You get so overwhelmed with a constant barrage of negatives that you become deaf to the possibilities God has in store for you.

Praise helps you to refocus on God's infinite reserves as well as on what He has done in your life. When everything goes wrong, you can always count on God's faithfulness, mercy, and kindness toward you in Jesus Christ. Often that truth is the only semblance of sanity that a person can cling to.

3. PRAISE REMINDS YOU OF GOD'S ABILITY TO PREVAIL IN YOUR LIFE

Praise results from recognizing that God is not only in control but that He "causes all things to work together for good to those who love God, to those who are called according to His purpose" (Romans 8:28). So praise is much more than some rosy, emotional high. Praise challenges your entire being—heart, mind, soul, and even body—to trust God with every problem you are facing. It includes a confident affirmation that God's hand will prevail in your life.

4. PRAISE STIMULATES GREATER FAITH FROM YOUR HEART

There's only one way to strengthen faith: You must test it; you must use it! Take God at His Word and prove that He is faithful: "Without faith it is impossible to please Him" (Hebrews 11:6). Because this biblical principle is true, don't be surprised when He allows the circumstances to develop in your life that *require you* to walk by faith. He is in control of your life, and He will take care of you.

One reason people are so hesitant to praise God in their dilemmas is that they're too busy blaming Him for everything that happens. They get in a bind because of some dumb thing they do and then complain to God. They blame Him for getting them into the jam in the first place. Does that sound like your story?

If you jump into water, you'll get wet. That's not God's fault. You made the decision to jump. But God allowed you the freedom to get in the water, and He provided the water. Your choices and their consequences are not God's fault. But He can use even bad circumstances for His glory and your growth, and He does know what is best for you. "In everything give thanks; for this is God's will for you in Christ Jesus" (1 Thessalonians 5:18).

5. PRAISE TORMENTS SATAN SO MUCH THAT HE WILL FLEE FROM YOU

If you're sick and tired of the devil wreaking havoc in your life, you don't have to take it anymore. When you determine to praise God in the midst of your circumstances, Satan flees. He wants out of there. He cannot stand to hear about the blood of Jesus Christ or God's name being praised because it reminds him of his doom. Praise is embedded in truth—eternal truth—and Satan can't bear to dwell in the light of the truth. Here's the way the apostle John put it.

And this is the judgment, that the Light has come into the world, and men loved the darkness rather than the Light, for their deeds were evil. For everyone who does evil hates the Light, and does not come to the Light for fear that his deeds should be exposed. But he who practices the truth comes to the Light, so that his deeds may be manifested as having been wrought in God. (John 3:19–21)

Praising God moves you from being on the defensive to becoming offensive in the realm of spiritual warfare. Just like in the game of football, your chances of scoring a touchdown are severely limited if your offensive team is never on the field. You have to have the ball to score. When you determine in your heart to praise God, you are transformed into an offensive agent on behalf of God. Satan is repelled from you: "Submit therefore to God. Resist the devil and he will flee from you" (James 4:7).

You can reopen the lines of communication with God when you acknowledge that He is in total control of your life. He is sovereign, meaning that He's totally in charge, whether you agree or not. He doesn't need your permission to be God. God can take you however He finds you, whatever condition you're in, and glorify Himself through you. He can do whatever He pleases, whenever He pleases, however He pleases, and He is always right. He never makes a mistake.

JOSEPH: A MAN OF PRAISE

A quick review of the life of Joseph shows that praising God in spite of horrible life circumstances can make a difference in an individual's life. Notice how Joseph responded in Genesis 39:20–23:

So Joseph's master took him and put him into the jail,

the place where the king's prisoners were confined; and
he was there in the jail. But the Lord was with Joseph
and extended kindness to him, and gave him favor in
the sight of the chief jailer. And the chief jailer committed to Joseph's charge all the prisoners who were in the
jail; so that whatever was done there, he was responsible for it. The chief jailer did not supervise anything
under Joseph's charge because the Lord was with him;
and whatever he did, the Lord made to prosper.

Being tossed in jail is only half of Joseph's story.
Consider also how Joseph's world fell apart on him:

- Joseph's brothers not only disowned him, but, in
  a fit of jealous rage, they plotted to murder him
  (Genesis 37:18).
- Ultimately his brothers sold him into slavery in
  Egypt (37:28).
- Joseph was falsely accused of rape and sexual
  harassment by Potiphar's wife (39:14). The result
  was that innocent, righteous Joseph was tossed
  into jail.

Talk about being victimized—Joseph is the textbook example. If anyone had it bad, he did. He lost his
homeland, his family, a high-ranking job, and all as a
result of doing the right thing.

Yet I cannot find one place in the Bible where
Joseph complained. He didn't moan. He didn't whine.
Neither did he count the days until God changed His
circumstances. In faith, Joseph stood up to the test and
trusted God to handle matters beyond his control. He
praised God in the midst of some devastating predica-
ments.

I know it's easy to complain. We all are tempted to complain when things don't go our way. The ridiculous thing is that we even complain when we get what we've been working for. When we get it, we discover that we don't want it. We weren't happy without it. Now we're unhappy *with it*. We just might be unhappy people, regardless of the circumstances. If that's the case for you, please know that God wants so much more for you (see 2 Chronicles 25:9).

God wants us to learn to trust Him, be thankful, and praise Him in the midst of our circumstances. Let Him have His way in your life. Ask God for wisdom, and He will let you know what you should be doing.

That's what you want, isn't it? Keep reading and you are going to understand how to win. It's about time you were a winner. Don't quit now. You're close to the finish line.

CONCLUDING PRINCIPLE:

Praising God puts the right perspective on your problems.

CHAPTER 7
FORGIVE
AND FORGET

I'm sure that a lot of people have hurt you. When someone goes through financial difficulties, usually much of the pain has been caused by others. I know that a lot of people have done me wrong. Once someone cheated me out of my interest in a company, and the company later was sold for several million dollars. My anger toward that person became the focus of my life. I would lie awake at night and think of what I could do to hurt that person. It was consuming me. I was going downhill. I had to get on top of the problem. I knew what to do—I had known all the time—but I did not want to give up my "rights." But eventually I knelt down and forgave the man.

Then, trying to do the right thing, I asked God to bless him. He did, which upset me even more. I finally had to surrender the whole thing to Jesus Christ and was, and am, done with it. *God* will deal with the person. My spiritual growth was put on hold the whole time this was going on. God would not hear me. My foundation was gone. I had nothing to build on.

Earlier we talked about laying the foundation for your new life in the Lord Jesus Christ. Laying this foundation properly will give you a way to go from the bottom of the barrel to the life of victory and success that God wants you to have. Once the proper foundation is laid, however, we must start building our life on that foundation.

THE CHALLENGE TO FORGIVE

God tells you to forgive others, meaning everyone, including yourself. Not tomorrow or next week, but now.

In order to understand and have God's success, you must get the issue of forgiveness behind you. It's like a cloud in your mind. You can't think clearly when you have something against another person. The inability to forgive, along with harboring bitterness and hatred, will consume you. You cannot be in full fellowship with the God of the Bible if you are unwilling to forgive. "If you forgive others for their transgressions, your heavenly Father will also forgive you. But if you do not forgive others, then your Father will not forgive your transgressions" (Matthew 6:14–15).

I know it might seem that others have wronged you, and they may have. That is not the question. The question is, Do you want to be free from the problems you are now having? Do you want to please God in your own life? Then forgive!

I have added words to some passages in the Bible that help me keep on track with my wife. (My words are in parentheses.)

For if you forgive others (including your wife) for their transgressions, your heavenly Father will also forgive you. But if you do not forgive others (including your wife), then your Father in heaven will not forgive your transgressions. (Matthew 6:14–15)

Do not judge (others, including your wife) so that you will not be judged. (7:1)

TED HAD PLENTY TO BE ANGRY ABOUT

When I met Ted, he was broke and living with a friend. His wife had divorced him several years before, leaving him embittered against the world. He had recently been cheated out of his share of a company that he helped to start. The company had done very well financially, so well in fact that it had outgrown Ted's ability to manage it. His partners had deceived him and cheated him out of more than half his stock, worth several million dollars.

Ted's anger and bitterness festered in him like an infected wound. He refused to trust anyone. He nose-dived into a depression caused by his own pity party. (Depression is often bitterness that is bottled up.)

Ted would have remained deeply depressed except for the efforts of a young pastor seeking to start a new church in the community. The energetic young man took time with Ted and eventually led him to faith in the Lord Jesus Christ. Once Ted realized that *his sins* were *forgiven*, he became free to forgive others. And that's exactly what he did.

When Ted forgave his former partners and put the entire fiasco behind, incredible things began to happen for him. Within eighteen months he and his wife were remarried, and he was in a new business of his own. I call that transformation a miracle. God unlocked the door of forgiveness in Ted's heart, and his life has been forever changed.

Are you hanging on to bitterness regarding things others have done to you? Let go! Forgive them. You are the one being hurt if you refuse to forgive. You can do it! The hurts won't disappear overnight, but they *will* begin to heal. If you forgive, no strings attached, you will experience more freedom than you've had in years.

PERSONAL COMMITMENT: Do it now! Make a list of everyone you can think of who has hurt you, and ask God to help you forgive them, all as an act of your will. Forgive them one by one, until the entire list is gone. You don't have to forgive them all in one day. Do as much as God gives you strength for. Take your time. This is so important that you need to take the time to think through each one you forgive. I have used a prayer something like this:

> Lord, by an act of my will I forgive [person's name] for [his/her specific sin against me]. I am still hurt but I want to be obedient to You and forgive others as a testimony to You of Your forgiveness of my sins.

I don't think you need to go to the individuals and tell them that you are forgiving them unless they have asked you to forgive them.

CONCLUDING PRINCIPLE:

*You cannot be forgiven
until you forgive.*

CHAPTER 8

TAKE RESPONSIBILITY FOR YOUR ACTIONS

I f you were bleeding from an arm wound, it would be useless to apply pressure on your leg or foot. You must apply pressure directly on the wound, no matter how painful it may be. The flow of blood must be successfully blocked, or you may bleed to death. Complaining, whining, or crying will contribute nothing to stopping the flow of blood. You must accept what the immediate threat is and neutralize it.

The same is true in the business world. Are you bleeding to death financially? Then you must take responsibility for what is happening, and take steps to stop it—fast.

Ed Harrison could have used that advice. There was a time when everything was going Ed's way. His home construction company had grown from a one-man operation to more than fifty employees. He earned more money than he ever dreamed of.

After years of struggling, Ed's turn for success had

arrived, and he intended to live it up. He began buying things he had always wanted, including new cars, a forty-two-foot houseboat, and a twin-engine airplane. He and his wife, Flo, took first-class vacations to Hawaii and France, fulfilling a cherished dream. Spending money, especially large sums, intoxicated Ed with feelings of success and power.

Then the whole thing began falling apart. After deciding that inflation was getting out of hand, the Federal Reserve began raising interest rates in 1974. Each increase staggered Ed, especially when the prime rose one full percent within twenty-four hours.

Housing sales collapsed, leaving Ed's dream world in big trouble. The rapid rise of interest rates made things tight for everyone, but it was worse for Ed. In fact, it was worse than it should have been. When housing sales evaporated, Ed became consumed with blaming the government. He retaliated with spite, hate, and bitterness, spending more time talking about what was wrong with the government than he did on correcting his problems. Old friends withdrew, unable to listen to all the complaining.

Even Flo had never seen him so out of control. She feared for him and anyone who got in his way. She pleaded with him to do something before it was too late. Finally, realizing saying anything was useless, Flo withdrew in silence.

As a result, he lost it all: home, cars, boat, airplane, and business. And he almost lost his wife. Ed was left with a handful of carpentry tools and a twelve-year-old pickup truck.

#1 PRIORITY: STOP THE BLEEDING BY TAKING RESPONSIBILITY

The number one priority of the man bleeding to death must be to stop the bleeding. Everything else must wait. Nothing else can take priority. For Ed to survive, he had to take emergency action to stop the financial hemorrhaging. In other words, he had to stop blaming others and take responsibility for what was happening.

Are you blaming someone or something else for your problems? What about God? Are you blaming Him? What about your wife, children, business partner, bank, or IRS? You can never get your life turned around until you stop blaming others. Even if your problems are truly the results of others' actions, it is not *their* problem—it's yours. And you are the one who needs to work to solve it.

Time after time when I counsel businesspeople, the issue of taking responsibility comes up. It may be an issue for you also. You must be "response-able" (able to respond) for your actions. Blaming someone or something else only masks the problem and delays the solution. Blaming is like applying pressure to your ankle when you have a deep arm wound—it doesn't work. Consider the following areas that God expects you to be responsible for:

- Your relationship with Him
- Finances
- Relationships
     with your parents
     with your brothers and sisters
     with your wife
     with your children

with your bank
with your suppliers
with other Christians, especially your
    church family

Are you ready to give account for how you have handled these areas? You should be, since God is going to hold you accountable for your actions. Genesis 3 tells the story of Adam and Eve eating the forbidden fruit in the Garden of Eden. God came looking for Adam and "called to the man, and said to him, 'Where are you?'" (Genesis 3:9).

The question today is not to Adam, but to you. Where are you? What's going on with you? Are you preventing God from blessing you by blaming others for your mistakes and decisions? Are you willing to take responsibility for your life and actions?

THE CAUSES OF IRRESPONSIBILITY

Some of the common root causes of irresponsibility are immaturity, ignorance, a victim mentality, circumstances, and no self-discipline.

IMMATURITY: REACTING LIKE A CHILD
WHEN THINGS DON'T GO YOUR WAY

Immaturity includes outbursts of anger, pouting, holding a grudge, or denial of the truth. I see this kind of reaction when people blame God for what has happened. The smallest things can trigger a fit of immaturity—bad weather, not being approved for a loan, or failing to close a sale at the price you were hoping for. Immaturity only complicates the problem-solving process.

IGNORANCE: NEVER KNOWING WHAT IT MEANS TO ASSUME RESPONSIBILITY FOR YOUR BEHAVIOR

As you think back over your life, perhaps you've never had a positive role model that demonstrated what responsible behavior looked like. You've heard the old saying "Ignorance is bliss." It may be in some situations, but it will never help to solve your problems.

VICTIM MENTALITY: ASSUMING THAT THERE ALWAYS HAS TO BE A VICTIM

There are times in life when things just happen or when you have to do certain things because circumstances require that they be done. You are not a victim. You're just being asked to be responsible.

I knew a man named Allen who thought he had been victimized. When his only brother died tragically, Allen discovered that he had been left out of the brother's will. Everything went to his sister, including a commercial building valued at more than $1 million. Allen felt rejected. Believing that he had been victimized, he became embittered and very depressed.

Two years later, more news came to light. Allen learned that hazardous materials had been processed in the building, and it was going to cost more than the building was worth to clean it up to EPA specifications. The prize had become a liability. When Allen realized that he could have been liable for hundreds of thousands of dollars, his bitterness and depression disappeared. And he realized his bitter spirit had hurt his relationship with his sister, so he called her and asked for her forgiveness. What a difference circumstances can make on our attitudes!

CIRCUMSTANCES: NOT HAVING
THE CHANCE TO BE RESPONSIBLE

Sometimes particular circumstances develop that take the decision making right out of your hands. Someone dies. Interest rates rise. The union strikes. The courts take away your rights to do something. The key is to take responsibility for *what is in your control* and trust God for things *beyond your control*.

NO SELF-DISCIPLINE: NOT WILLING
TO MAKE THE ROUGH DECISIONS

You want the easy way out, or you want to avoid conflict. You're not willing to work hard. You're not willing to do what is necessary to get the job done. You procrastinate in dealing with people and problems. You're not willing to get out of your comfort zone.

Some of these thoughts may rub you the wrong way. But there are definite rewards that result from being the responsible person God wants you to be:

Peace of mind. You've done everything you can do, and that's all God asks you to do. Others may still be upset with you, but there's a special, inward peace that comes from knowing that you are being a good steward of what God has entrusted to you.

Knowing that God can trust you. Because you've been faithful with a few things (Matthew 25:21), God will entrust larger things to you. He has tested you and found you faithful; now He can trust you with the big things.

Having the trust of your family and friends. They will trust you and count on you because you have proven that you are dependable. You are a man of your word.

You say what you mean and mean what you say, and like Jesus you keep your promises.

Being proactive with problems. You don't turn your head when difficult or painful issues arise. You wisely recognize the threat and move aggressively to "nip problems in the bud." And what a joy comes from knowing that you have dealt with issues responsibly and don't have to carry them around with you everywhere.

Here are some practical steps you can follow to grow in taking responsibility for your life:

Spend time alone with God. The voices of men will compete for "time and space" in your mind. You need solitude . . . just you and Jesus. Discover why He calls Himself the "good shepherd" in John 10:14.

Make an absolute commitment to do what God says. Invite the Holy Spirit to direct your Bible study to the specific passages you need to hear.

Ask God to show you the areas you need to work on. Be specific. Expect Him to reveal to you what you need to do to get things right. Study Psalm 139 in preparation for this step.

Ask others to help you in these areas by committing to be accountable to someone.

Be prepared for a rough ride. No one said this journey would be easy, but is there a realistic alternative?

The good news is that you and God can accomplish this task. You have already won this battle because you are ready to stop hurting. It's time to get on with a life that is filled with joy and peace, the highest quality of life that comes from doing the will of the Father.

CONCLUDING PRINCIPLE:

Blaming others delays your progress; taking responsibility hastens it.

ESTABLISHING A NEW DIRECTION

CHAPTER 9
WHERE ARE YOU?

One of the most crucial things for you to know in life is where you are: where you are spiritually; where you are in your relationships with your mate, children, friends, peers; and where you are financially. It is impossible to plan a successful trip unless you know your starting point and your destination. The best road map in the world cannot help you unless you know where you are and where you want to go.

Most people, including me, get trapped into wanting *something*, without really understanding what they want. I am quick to say, "Let's do it!" without thinking through the results. Nevertheless, if you want to go somewhere, you must take action. If you want to get out of the hole you are in, you must take action.

Where are you on the road map of life? Where do you want to go? Connect the two with the shortest line and you have made a major step in the right direction. There has to be a starting point in order for you to measure progress. Now is the time to stop and determine where you are in your life. Look at each area of your life, including your work, your relationships or your marriage, your parenthood, your finances, your walk

with the Lord, and your relationship to your church.
They are connected, you know. If you only deal with
one area, your problems may continue to grow.

To help you gain a clearer picture of your life, I
have provided some evaluation forms in Appendix B.
The purpose is to help you take a long hard look at
yourself and your condition.

Can you tell anyone today where you are in all the
areas mentioned above? We are just stewards of our
lives, meaning the Lord has left you responsible for
these areas. We can't hide anything from Him.

Hebrews 4:13 states, "And there is no creature hid-
den from His sight, but all things are open and laid bare
to the eyes of Him with whom we have to do." And
Romans 14:12 says, "So then each of us will give an
account of himself to God."

KNOW WHERE YOU ARE FINANCIALLY

Let me stop here and talk about something that
will keep coming up. Cash flow. Have you noticed how
many businesses have "cash flow problems"? Most of
the time it really means they are broke or close to it.
The reason most people say they have a cash flow problem when they ask for help is that they don't have a
clue where they are financially. Most don't even know
whether they are making a profit or not.

The person who asked me to work with Fred told
me he was a very committed Christian. His business
was doing very well but he was having cash flow problems—something I was familiar with.

When I got to his offices and asked to see the current financial statement, he said his staff was working
on it. So I asked for the first six months' statement, and

he replied that they were just now working on it as well (this was October).

I knew right then why the man was having cash flow problems—he didn't know how much money he was spending! When Fred finally got his books up to date, he discovered he was $280,000 in the hole. The business was closed within thirty days by the major supplier. Fred didn't know where he was financially, and he paid a terrible price as a result.

Proverbs 27:23–24 says, "Know well the condition of your flocks, and pay attention to your herds; for riches are not forever, nor does a crown endure to all generations."

Let me tell you about someone else. Jimmy had never owned a business before. He was contacted by a very sharp, but dishonest, salesman. He told Jimmy that he could make more than $2,000 a month on each of the three convenience stores he wanted to sell.

Without any planning, research, or further investigation, Jimmy made a down payment using all of his savings and signed a note for hundreds of thousands of dollars. Without taking inventory or anything else, Jimmy took over. Thirty days later he knew he was in trouble because he was unable, out of cash flow, to replace the stock he had sold.

He kept the three stores for almost a year before he was forced into bankruptcy. Jimmy never knew where he was, even in the end.

By the way, Jimmy did not need more money. He was already making enough to have a good lifestyle, help others, and build a savings account.

WHERE ARE YOU WITH YOUR MARRIAGE?

Charles and his wife walked into my office one day and said they needed some advice on what to do about a business decision they had to make.

After listening to Charles for almost an hour, I turned to his wife and asked her what she thought about it. She told me without emotion, "I don't care what he does, I probably won't be there, anyway." Charles almost fell out of his chair.

As it turned out, Charles thought he needed help with a business decision when what he really needed was to start including his wife and work as a team. He did not really know what was going on with his wife. He had never asked her. He was about to lose his wife without knowing why.

This story had a positive ending. Charles really did love his wife, and when he started including her in everything, he discovered she was a good counselor in helping him make decisions. He didn't need any help; he was living with a great source of wisdom and insight —his wife!

The point is that Charles did not know the condition of his marriage. Most men don't. We are going to talk about that more later on. But ironically, when he started including her insights in his decision making, the secondary problem—finances—also turned around.

When you finish reading this book, I challenge you to work on the forms in Appendix B. You will understand better how to discover *where you are* in your life. Don't limit yourself to the forms. If you need more room get some blank paper.

CONCLUDING PRINCIPLE:

If you don't know where you are, you can't get there from here.

CHAPTER 10

WHERE DO YOU WANT TO GO?

The definition of success depends on whom you're talking to. What one person considers success may not amount to much to the next person. Success might mean something very basic to you right now, like surviving another week or eating another meal.

But as you plan your future, sooner or later you'll have to come to grips with what true success means. What does it mean to you? And is your picture of success consistent with God's Word?

To help you gather your thoughts, let me give you an example of a Christian whose life reflects a godly definition of success. Ike lives with his family in the Midwest. I had the occasion to meet him when I needed help on a project, and he was referred to me with very high remarks. The project would not have required a great deal of time and offered substantial money for Ike.

When I contacted him with the proposal, he responded with "no way." He had no time to spare in his schedule.

Curious, I probed him to learn more and discovered that Ike was happily married with two children.

Then he told me what his schedule was each week.

"On Monday night I am committed to discipling three men on how to run their businesses based on biblical principles.

"On Tuesday night, my wife and I teach a new believers' Bible study at the church.

"Wednesday night is family night at the church. We eat supper there, attend the pastor's Bible study, and both my wife and I stay for choir practice.

"I keep Thursday night set aside for my eight-year-old daughter. We generally go window shopping or whatever she wants to do. I let her decide. Sometimes we just talk.

"On Friday nights I go with my son. We play ball, get a hot dog, or do something just for men.

"Saturday's a catch-up day for us at the house, and we try to accomplish some things together like yardwork, repair work, and cleaning. We try to finish by lunch time, leaving the afternoon free for some type of family outing. Then on Saturday night, I take my wife out for a date. I've been dating her on Saturday nights since she was sixteen, and I'm not about to stop now.

"And Sunday is the Lord's day. We've given that day over to worship and service through our church family. I'd like to help you, but I don't have extra time."

For Ike, success meant being deeply involved in the lives of his family and church. But I was curious about his idea of material success. After all, he had bills to pay, the same as you and me. When I questioned him about that, he told me that he had more than $200,000 in CDs in the bank, and he gave more than *33 percent* of his income to the Lord's work. I was impressed.

Indeed, Ike's lifestyle made such an impression on me that I wanted to know more. Curiosity had gotten the best of me, and besides, I get blessed by hearing how God is at work in the lives of others.

But I wasn't prepared for what Ike was about to tell me.

"I've always wanted to do things God's way," Ike began. "I had been a carpet installer for over eight years when I felt God's prompting to go into business for myself. I could see where I could provide for my family better that way compared to working for someone else.

"The book of Proverbs encouraged me to seek godly counsel, so I set up an appointment with a retired businessman in our church named Zach and asked him to teach me how to run a business based on the Bible.

"Zach said he would pray about it, and in a couple of weeks he returned to me with this offer. 'I'll give you all the information you need to be a success,' he told me, 'but under the following three conditions.

"'First, you must agree to meet with me every week on Thursday for three hours over the next six months. If you miss even one meeting, the deal's off.

"'Second, you must agree not to come back to me for advice. When I'm through, I'm through. I want you to be dependent on God and the Bible, not me. I will teach you everything I know to run a business and be a success in life. After that, it will be up to you to learn it and live it.

"'Third, you must agree to do exactly what I tell you for the first two years after you start the business. After that, if you want to make changes you can. But you must agree to do it my way for the first two years.'"

Ike told me he accepted the offer. "After six months

of hard work, training, and sacrifices by my family, I was on my own. I not only had Zach's blessing but when I had finished everything he had told me to do, he also gave me a check for $10,000 with his blessing. He was sure I would be a success because Jesus Christ was so real in my life and work. I was both honored and humbled by Zach's confidence and by God's blessing."

The new business involved selling and installing carpet. Ike told me all Zach had taught him about setting up the business. The steps Ike agreed to follow during at least the first two years in the business were the following:

- ✔ rent a 10' X 10' office
- ✔ use an answering service with beepers
- ✔ use a bookkeeping service
- ✔ do not rent a warehouse or a forklift
- ✔ do not purchase carpet displays; rather, use the free samples provided through the carpet mills
- ✔ don't let customers come to you; rather, go to them in their homes where they can match colors with the carpet samples
- ✔ rent a 4' X 12' space on the floor of the trucking company for storage until the carpet is installed
- ✔ buy and sell in cash only
- ✔ have no accounts receivable or payable
- ✔ get a deposit when the sale is made
- ✔ be present when the carpet installers are about to finish, making sure the customer is satisfied with both the quality of carpet and the installation
- ✔ correct any problems on the spot
- ✔ don't leave the installation without a check
- ✔ don't drive a car less than five years old

- ✔ don't change residences for the next five years
- ✔ don't change your lifestyle, regardless of how much money you make, for five years
- ✔ put all the money you make over $10,000 into savings, but only after you first tithe to the Lord
- ✔ when your income has reached the same level as it was prior to starting the business, help someone else start his business
- ✔ never work on Sunday; worship the Lord on His day
- ✔ be accountable to other men for all areas of your life
- ✔ plan a quality date with your wife once a week
- ✔ commit to a quality quiet time with the Lord every day
- ✔ never violate God's Word for any reason, even if that means starting over

Ike continued, "I did exactly what Zach told me to do. It took a while to see results, but the business eventually grew stronger. By the end of the first year, I was making more than I did before starting the business. In fact, things were going so well that I didn't dare change anything. I still live in the same house and my car is seven years old. I still live on the same amount of money and operate on $10,000 cash. Anything above that, I do what Zach told me to do. I put it in the bank after I give the Lord His tithe.

"And you know what?" Ike asked me. "I am blessed by God with so much peace and joy, I have to pinch myself to make sure I'm not dreaming."

I asked him why he didn't expand and get a secretary. "Why? Besides, I'm not smart enough to do better than I'm doing now," he replied.

Now I'd say that Ike is an excellent example of success. Ike is doing it God's way. He's smart enough to live within his limitations, and he's humble enough to realize he doesn't know it all. He is literally a student of his business. He obeyed God and received the blessing of success. Ike did his part, and God did His part. And Ike is now wise enough to realize "who does what" in that equation. He knows that God called him to faithfully work the process and trust God for the results. Know what? It works.

WHAT'S YOUR IDEA OF SUCCESS?

So what is success for you? When you reach the top of the career ladder you're climbing, will you be successful? How much is enough for you? Do you know what your limitations are? Are you humble enough to take godly counsel from someone else?

Take the time to write down what success means to you. Consider all the areas of your life, not just business. Carefully review what you say in the planning worksheets at the back of the book (Appendixes B and C). Are your plans dictated by greed, or are you truly desiring what God wants?

Think through what constitutes success for you, and as you do, don't forget to identify the key values driving your definition of success. Make notes below and date them. You may refer back to them in future years to update them or completely change them.

This is my brief definition of success:

_____

_____

_____

_____

_____

_____

_____

_____

_____   _____

YOUR SIGNATURE   DATE

CONCLUDING PRINCIPLE:

> *If you have not
> defined success,
> how will you know
> when you achieve it?*

CHAPTER 11

WHAT WOULD JESUS DO?

I t's not always easy to understand exactly what Jesus would do in a given situation. Discovering His will takes a great deal of prayer, listening, and most of all a willingness to obey.

It was July of 1992, and my wife Janet and I had, not one, but *four* mega-decisions to make, each loaded with long-term consequences. For weeks I had been praying for God to shed some light, for Him to grant a breakthrough, some direction, something. But I had not a word from the Lord. Nothing.

But this particular morning was different. My frustration boiled over into a determination to hear from God. Enough was enough. Like Jacob in Genesis 32:26, I was motivated to wrestle with the Lord in prayer until I had an answer.

"GOD, I NEED AN ANSWER!"

Have you ever gotten to a point where you don't even care *what* the answer to your prayer is, so long as you *do get an answer* from the Lord? Well, that's where I was. I was determined to hear from God. Time was running out for me, and I had decisions that had to be made one way or the other.

I rolled out of bed, made my way into the den, and got down on my knees before God with my face to the floor. I prayed something like this: "Lord, I know that You have the answers to my problems and I have come for those answers. I am going to stay here until I get them. I will do whatever You say. I am not shopping for answers to fit what I want. I want what You want."

Each of the four decisions offered two clear choices: either one way or the other. Based on the intensity of my resolve, I expected the Lord to move right that moment and make His answer clear. But it didn't happen that way. Instead, I endured forty-five minutes of absolute silence. Nothing.

But something happened to me during that silence. As I look back, I can see now that God was waiting for me to listen, not with my head, but with my heart. I said I was willing to wait for an answer, but I expected Him to answer immediately, on my timetable. When my heart was finally tuned in to His Spirit, the action began.

And it wasn't the answer I was expecting. Quoting from my journal, here's what God spoke to my heart that morning: "Van, you have the wrong issues. I am the issue in your life. Listen to Me. Seek My counsel and My ways. Follow and obey Me."

That's all. I knew the answer was what I really needed, though it wasn't what I had asked. The pressure evaporated and I was at peace. And you know what was so odd? God *did not* give me the specific answers to the decisions I was facing. Instead, He gave me a larger principle I needed to learn. It was a principle that helped me to see all of my decisions, in fact my whole life, in a new light. As I read and reread what I had written down, I knew He had brought perfect focus to the real issue in my life: my relationship with Him.

Jesus said, "Abide in Me, and I in you. As the branch cannot bear fruit of itself unless it abides in the vine, so neither can you unless you abide in Me. I am the vine, you are the branches; he who abides in Me and I in him, he bears much fruit, for apart from Me you can do nothing" (John 15:4–5).

Having a prayer answered by God with a principle is like receiving a wrapped gift at Christmas. You have to unwrap it, open it, and use it to fully receive the benefit of the gift. That's what I had to do with the principle God gave to me. In fact, you may be wondering how His message could be of any help at all.

But as I meditated on what God said, here's the application He helped me to see. *My challenge was to do whatever Jesus would do.* For each of the decisions I was facing, I had to determine what Jesus would do, then do it. Like a vine supplying all that a branch needs, Jesus simply wanted to live His life through me. He wanted me to think His thoughts, say His words, love with His love, and do what He would do.

That may sound simplistic. After all, Jesus never married, dealt with technology, or sold a business . . . and not every question is black and white. Giving fifty dollars to either of two apparently worthy charities may be one example. Or deciding whether to stay in a present job or work for oneself . . . or to bypass both options and instead send out résumés to get a new job. Maybe either is an equally valid option. But the question remains legitimate, because Jesus is living His life through you, and He wants you to seek the choices He would make and to make choices the way He would make them.

Jesus said, "If anyone serves Me, he must follow Me; and where I am, there My servant will be also; if anyone serves Me, the Father will honor him" (John 12:26).

Paul wrote in 2 Timothy 3:10, "But you followed my teaching, conduct, purpose, faith, patience, love, perseverance."

My prayer experience was an interesting paradox. God didn't specifically make my decisions for me, yet, in a broader way, He did. I thought I was really chasing down the important issues in my life until God reminded me, "I am your issue, Van. Concentrate on Me, and I'll supply what you need each day." Could that be the real issue in *your* life as it was in mine?

And now, I really want God's answers. I want to know that God hears me when I pray. I want God's will in my life because it's the best for me. Do you want the same?

It's true that you face incredibly tough decisions and situations in your life. But you contribute to the problem by mixing your personal agendas and your will with what God says. You want both. You want God's best but you want to get it your way. And of course, that immediate conflict of interest results in a shutdown.

Jesus teaches, "Any kingdom divided against itself is laid waste; and a house divided against itself falls" (Luke 11:17).

James tells us, "But if any of you lacks wisdom, let

him ask of God, who gives to all generously and without reproach, and it will be given to him. But he must ask in faith without any doubting, for the one who doubts is like the surf of the sea, driven and tossed by the wind. For that man ought not to expect that he will receive anything from the Lord, being a double-minded man, unstable in all his ways" (James 1:5–8).

Your life will be greatly simplified if you would determine to do what Jesus would do and say in each situation you face. After all, that's literally what it means to call Him Lord. He's the Boss. He calls the shots. Are you ready to live His way? Are you ready to relinquish control of your life, your future, your career, your everything to Him?

I read a book four or five times a year called *In His Steps* by Charles M. Sheldon (Keats Publishing, Inc.) because it helps me to reflect on doing things the way Jesus would. I need that encouragement because most of the time I would not have thought of the way Jesus would do something. The book is challenging, motivational, and inspirational, and I encourage you to get a copy for yourself and read it through. It's so popular that more than 60 million copies have been sold.

So think about this. What would Jesus do if He were in your situation right now? How would He relate to the people in your world: your creditors, your family, or your business associates? How would Jesus respond to the setbacks and disappointments you have faced? Perhaps you have been betrayed by those who were the most trusted people in your life—how would Jesus respond to them?

The answers to what Jesus would do can be found in God's written Word. God supplies the Bible so "that the man of God may be adequate, equipped for every good work" (2 Timothy 3:17).

Now you may be saying to yourself, "Yeah, but I won't find the specific answer I need." But by studying the Bible, you will learn how Jesus handled difficult situations. God will provide the insight you need, but you must provide the obedience.

WHEN WALLY DID IT GOD'S WAY

Take Wally, for example. Wally had everything going for him. His income had been over $100,000 for years. He lived in the nicest neighborhood in town; he drove luxury cars; he gave to God's work generously. His family had plenty of love and encouragement to share with others.

And then disaster struck his business, leaving him literally penniless. His family lost everything, including their home. With no place for them to go, the church family had to take care of them.

How would you have responded? Maybe you're in a similar situation right now. Here's what Wally did. He gathered his wife and two teenagers for a family meeting and led them in praise and worship before God. As Wally prayed, he thanked God for his family's health and the provisions made by the church family, and he confessed his faith that God would lead them through the extreme difficulties the family was facing. He asked God for grace to adapt to the changes they had to make, for new employment opportunities, for wisdom to know what Jesus would do, and, in particular, for joy. Deep-down joy, knowing that the Bible teaches believers to rejoice in everything.

Scripture says, "In everything give thanks; for this

is God's will for you in Christ Jesus" (1 Thessalonians 5:18) and "Consider it all joy, my brethren, when you encounter various trials . . ." (James 1:2). Wally took those verses seriously.

Wally discovered God's insight on giving thanks in the midst of adversity, and he determined to obey what he learned. The results of his obedience were life-changing.

I want you to know that God answered Wally's prayers, some more quickly than others. For instance, Wally's family began to experience joy as a result of his prayers. But there was more. The crushing weight of their burdens was lifted and they had real hope. Each sensed the Lord Jesus *right there in the room* with them, ministering to their battered emotions, taking away their fears.

Answers to Wally's prayers for new work were not immediate, but God was working. Curiously, Wally's joy became the catalyst to his new employment. He didn't know it, but his joy and faith caught the eye of a fellow Christian in his church family, a man Wally hadn't met before. The man observed Wally's attitude in the midst of the crisis. Liking what he saw, the man offered Wally a night auditor's job in a motel he owned, even though the salary was only $100 a week.

With a thankful heart, Wally took the job, believing that's what Jesus wanted him to do in spite of the low salary. It was a wise step. With the passing of time, the man hired Wally to run the entire conglomerate of motels.

Although Wally's prayer for joy was answered immediately, his prayers for new employment directions took more time for God to answer. The key, however, was in Wally's commitment to respond to the adversity the way Jesus would—with joy and thanks-giving. It was the evidence of that obedience that caught the eye of his future employer.

Now you may be saying to yourself, "Who is this Van Thurston guy, some kind of nut, telling me that I should be *thankful* for all this chaos and trouble I'm having in my life?"

Look *beyond* the storm. Give thanks to God who will lead you through the storm and who will be glori-fied by your response to the storm. A tragedy remains a tragedy until you trust God (Romans 8:28).

Deciding to follow Jesus may prompt you to praise God in some unusual situations. And that decision may also prompt you to make unusual choices (at least from a worldly point of view).

WHEN NORMAN DID THE UNTHINKABLE

For instance, you may not believe what Norman did five years ago. Norman ran a very profitable business that thrived on the inventions he brought to the indus-try. After much toil and dedication, he compiled a mail-ing list with several thousand names that produced a 33 percent purchase rate when he unveiled new products.

Norman's executive vice president, Bill, was a Chris-tian who consistently made well over $75,000 a year. Bill's greedy appetite for more drove him to dishonesty. The perfect opportunity to steal came when Norman was on a three-week business trip in Europe. Bill made his move, cleverly stealing some of Norman's new prod-ucts along with his lucrative mailing list. His intent was to start his own business.

When Norman learned of this, he was crushed not

only by the loss of business he suffered but, more importantly, by Bill's deception. Believing the biblical instruction that he should not sue a Christian brother, however, Norman refused to take legal action against Bill.

People couldn't understand why Norman didn't go after him. "You should put him away," they said. Nail his hide to the wall. "Do unto others *before* they do unto you," said one person.

At first it appeared that Bill had gotten away with the theft. But initial successes soon soured, and within a year, Bill was in trouble financially. When Norman learned that Bill's cash flow problem was acute, he was prompted by God to respond. He called Bill and offered to help. Even though Bill was flabbergasted, he accepted the offer. But the business continued to worsen to the point that he eventually lost it. And guess what Norman did? He offered Bill his old job back as senior VP.

Is that what Norman should have done? I can't say for sure, but one thing is clear. Norman took seriously the admonition of Jesus to forgive others. What would you have done? And better yet, what would Jesus have done? What passages can you find in Scripture that illustrate what Jesus would have done?

Can you imagine what would happen in the American business world if every Christian simply resolved to do everything the way Jesus would do it? What would happen in your world? What would happen in your life *today* if you resolved to "walk the walk and talk the talk" of Jesus in every matter, with no compromises?

You may be thinking, "Yeah, but that's too much of a price to pay. I have too much to lose." Do you? There's great freedom when you're at the bottom of the barrel in life. At the bottom you don't have anything left to lose. Nothing left to protect. No more assets. No more reputation. No more future to count on. Nothing's a "given" anymore. And if doing things your own way landed you at the bottom, maybe it's time to try living another way—Christ's way.

The good news is that Christ's way is the best way. God does some of His greatest, most dramatic work in the lives of people who are scraping the bottom of the barrel simply because they are open and willing. Are you?

BENEFITS OF FOLLOWING GOD'S EXAMPLE

Here are some of the benefits from committing to live your life following the model of Jesus.

1. There is freedom. You can toss to the side all the issues that used to bind you. Jesus said, "So if the Son makes you free, you will be free indeed" (John 8:36). He calls the shots. His role is to be a wise shepherd; your role is to listen carefully to Him and obey what you hear. The result is incredible freedom. Trying to fill God's shoes by calling all the shots yourself is rather exhausting, isn't it?

Committing to live the way Jesus does will open the door to a clear conscience for you. You'll be able to sleep in peace again at night. And, since you won't have anything to hide, you can be transparent with others.

2. You establish a credible witness for the Gospel.

Do people respect you for your work? If not, it may be because you have adopted habits, attitudes, and behaviors that are simply not godly. Follow Christ. No other life has had the impact on humanity that He has. He's worthy of your trust and obedience. God will restore you as a credible witness because your actions will be both wise and honorable. And it feels great to be respected.

3. You cultivate self-worth based on what Jesus says, not what the world says about you. Let's face it. When you're constantly attempting to please everyone else in your world, you can never do enough.

In contrast, through faith in Christ, you become a new creature (2 Corinthians 5:17). You still inhabit the same old body, but praise God, there's a new person inside. The Bible says God was willing to pay the price of His only Son, Jesus Christ, in order to make you part of His family.

Or do you not know that your body is a temple of the Holy Spirit who is in you, whom you have from God, and that you are not your own? For you have been bought with a price: therefore glorify God in your body. (1 Corinthians 6:19–20)

And if you address as Father the One who impartially judges according to each one's work, conduct yourselves in fear during the time of your stay on earth; knowing that you were not redeemed with perishable things like silver or gold from your futile way of life inherited from your forefathers, but with precious blood, as of a lamb unblemished and spotless, the blood of Christ. (1 Peter 1:17–19)

Now if you want, you can choose to continue that nonsense of resting your self-worth on worldly measures of success. But look where that plan has brought you today. Do you really want more of the same?

As an alternative, you can choose the life of Jesus Christ. Maybe you've done that before. But then again, maybe you've never really launched into the deep with Him.

What will you do? When will you start? Will you continue choosing what you want . . . or what God wants? Why not get alone with God somewhere and pray for His insight? The choice is yours. In love and in the spirit of truth, I challenge you to decide today.

_____ *With no strings attached, I have decided to live my life the way Jesus would live. I resolve to search the Bible daily to learn how.*

_____ *I choose to do it my way. I'm not convinced yet that the way of Christ is for me.*

_____   _____

YOUR SIGNATURE   DATE

Others with whom I shared my decision:

_____   _____

_____   _____

_____   _____

_____   _____

CONCLUDING PRINCIPLE:

*Do everything the
way Jesus would.*

CHAPTER 12
WHY YOU NEED A PLAN

I f I don't *plan* an activity, it usually never happens. Is it that way with you too? During the week, I'll catch myself making mental notes about all the things I need to get done the following Saturday. But if I never get around to making a plan to do them, my thoughts are either forgotten or pushed to the side by more urgent or more interesting matters when Saturday arrives.

Plans do not only provide you with a sense of direction; they also help you distinguish between "necessary" activities and distractions. Without a plan, you're likely to slide into a totally reactive mode in your life, where others control your time, your energy, the direction of your work, your cash flow—every aspect of living. Consequently, others also control the *results* of all these areas.

If that's true of you, and you're sick of that kind of lifestyle, then you're ready to accept the discipline of planning in your life. You need a career plan, a plan for your family, a financial plan, a plan to get out of debt, a plan for leisure time, and even a plan for the day God has given you today. If that sounds like too many plans to handle, then you also need to *plan* to make time to *plan*. That's right. You need time just to sit still and think about your life, your schedule, your month, and your day. Make notes; fill in your calendar; get with your spouse and compare your schedules. If you're like me, if you don't plan something, it usually doesn't get done. Thus, priority activities usually have a plan behind them.

GOD HAS PLANS; SHOULDN'T YOU?

Everywhere you look in Scripture, you'll find evidence that God is a God who plans. Just look at what God has to say about His planning.

> "For I know the plans that I have for you," declares the Lord, "plans for welfare and not for calamity to give you a future and a hope." (Jeremiah 29:11)

> Many are the plans in a man's heart, but the counsel of the Lord, it will stand. (Proverbs 19:21)

Of course, Scripture never indicates that plans of any kind are better than no plans at all. God only blesses plans that are wise, have integrity, and are made according to biblical principles. Here are some things Scripture says about human planning.

> But the noble man devises noble plans; and by noble plans he stands. (Isaiah 32:8)

> Woe to those who deeply hide their plans from the Lord, and whose deeds are done in a dark place, and they say, Who sees us? or Who knows us? (Isaiah 29:15)

> Prepare plans by consultation, and make war by wise guidance. (Proverbs 20:18)

> Commit your works to the Lord and your plans will be established. (Proverbs 16:3)

God is a God who plans and who wants us to make plans also. In His grace, wisdom, and providence, He has everything worked out for us. He has a master plan for your life that includes personal planning on your part. He wants you to know and understand where you are going.

I know you may not be interested in a ten-year plan right now, or, for that matter, even a one-year plan. You may be thinking to yourself, *What I need is a plan for buying groceries today, or paying the back rent, or keeping my kids in clothes.* I understand that. If you're hurting, I know that a ten-year plan for your life won't put food on the table today.

But you do need to start working on a direction. Face it. Failing to plan is planning to fail. You need to get before God in prayer and then make some basic decisions about your life.

I wish I could count the number of times I've counseled with people in financial difficulty who had no plans at all. Beyond deliverance from their immediate circumstances, they had no plans for the rest of their lives . . . none whatsoever. As a result, they are likely going to repeat the same mistake over and over. They'll get a little money and then it's back to the old ways. I don't want that to happen to you.

I remember one man I counseled who was $200,000 in the hole. He was perplexed, however, because he had met his annual goal of selling $2 million worth of furniture. When I asked him what his *profit* goal was, he said he didn't have one. Do you see? His only plan was to sell $2 million worth of furniture. He was not focused on the real objective: *selling $2 million worth of furniture with a profit of $150,000.* Selling the furniture wouldn't do him any good *unless he made a profit.*

WHAT PLANNING IS *NOT*

Before I show you some areas that require planning, let me be clear about what planning is *not.*

Planning is not the same as wishing. If your heart is set on being rich, or famous, or powerful, or in control, or to have a certain person or thing, or to have some kind of status in the world, that's not planning. That's wishing. You can literally wish your life away. Isn't it true that most of the things you wish for stem from having the wrong value system or just being unhappy with what God has given you at this time in your life?

For instance, most of the hundreds of people I have talked to over the years, when I asked them what they need to do to solve their problems, said, "make a lot of money." In fact, I can remember only three who literally needed more money. With most, the problem was not a lack of money. That was only a symptom of a larger and much different problem.

Neither does planning mean that you set out on a course of action and refuse to make adjustments even when your original plan isn't working. Wise business-people begin with a plan, but they know how to read changing circumstances and make the necessary adjustments. Planning doesn't mean arbitrarily setting a plan in motion and then sticking your head in the sand. Rather, successful planning makes allowance for ongoing evaluations and adjustments. When an airplane flies from one city to another, the pilot has a flight plan, but he must constantly monitor conditions affecting his flight in order to safely arrive at his destination. In fact, sometimes weather conditions at his planned destination are such that he can't land there but is rerouted to another city. Wise plans can also be flexible plans.

Neither does planning imply that you set out on a course of action without first seeking wise counsel or being open to God's correction as your plans develop. "Where there is no guidance, the people fall, but in abundance of counselors there is victory" (Proverbs 11:14).

When I talk about planning, I mean prayerfully considering the major directions of your life. I mean directing your effort in a way that will give you the desired result. Another way to put it is to decide in advance what you are going to focus your life on so you will get what you really want.

Your life never stands still. You're either headed toward your life's purpose or wandering away from it. You're going in one direction or the other. So why not develop a road map for your life based on God's principles that will take you where *He* wants you to be?

Listen to the wisdom of the Lord Jesus. "For which one of you, when he wants to build a tower, does not first sit down and calculate the cost to see if he has enough to complete it?" (Luke 14:28). What will it cost you to live out the road map of your life? Do you even have a written plan in place?

Most people who wind up in financial struggles get there because they haven't developed a plan for their lives. They don't even know what they want, much less are they organized to get it. They just react to their particular circumstances or environment as though such elements were totally beyond their control. Beyond wanting a lot of money, many simply lack lifelong direction and purpose. What about you? What are you living for?

Someone once asked John D. Rockefeller how much money he wanted. His answer was simple: "Just a little bit more." I think that describes the attitude of a lot of people in America right now. They want just a little bit more, a little bit newer, a little bit bigger, a little bit different, or a little bit prettier. Let me ask you this: Is the real plan for your life right now just trying to get more? Is that what it's all about?

The truth is that God will give you everything you need, every possible good gift, and blessings beyond anything you could ever desire, if you simply plan according to His Word. God wants you to be blessed. But listen to your heart. He will not give you things that will draw you away from Him.

Planning involves thinking and praying through what God wants for you and where you plan to be six months, a year, and even five years from now. Like I discussed in an earlier chapter, the process of planning begins with your commitment to Jesus Christ. There's no need to waste time climbing a ladder if it's leaning against the wrong building. But once you've made that important commitment to Jesus Christ as your Lord and Savior, then it's time to plan.

And when you plan, the wise thing to do is plan

with God's thoughts and wisdom in mind. Below are listed four key principles that will help you develop your plans. Study them carefully as you contemplate God's leading in your life.

#1 — THE PRINCIPLE OF PROFITABILITY

Will your spiritual life profit because of your plans? When your goals are met, will you be better or worse off in your daily walk with Jesus? Are you expecting God to bless a plan that will weaken your relationship with Him?

The apostle Paul writes, "All things are lawful for me, but not all things are profitable. All things are lawful for me, but I will not be mastered by anything" (1 Corinthians 6:12).

#2 — THE PRINCIPLE OF EXCESS

"Therefore, since we have so great a cloud of witnesses surrounding us, let us also lay aside every encumbrance and the sin which so easily entangles us, and let us run with endurance the race that is set before us, fixing our eyes on Jesus, the author and perfecter of faith" (Hebrews 12:1–2a).

If your plans come to pass, will they "add baggage" by complicating your walk with the Lord, or lighten your load in life? A sure self-test of this principle is whether you find yourself worrying more or experiencing more of God's peace and contentment.

#3 — THE PRINCIPLE OF ENSLAVEMENT

Will the fulfillment of your plans leave you free or will it put you in bondage to something or someone else? Will you be free to respond if God changes your circumstances, or will the fulfillment of your plans leave you desperately out of control? "For by what a man is overcome, by this he is enslaved" (2 Peter 2:19b).

#4 — THE PRINCIPLE OF ENCROACHMENT

Will you violate your sense of obedience to God, or encroach upon His revealed written Word, in order to fulfill your plans? God has never blessed sin and never will. Willful sin sent His Son to the cross! If you can find biblical truths that contradict your plans, you might as well think of another plan of action.

"There is a way which seems right to a man, but its end is the way of death" (Proverbs 14:12).

"For what will it profit a man if he gains the whole world and forfeits his soul? Or what will a man give in exchange for his soul?" (Matthew 16:26).

To help you develop plans for your future, I have included several forms in Appendix C at the back of the book. And don't forget this: When you make plans, your spouse must be in agreement. Let me caution you about overpowering your mate. *Don't.* Intimidating your lifelong companion won't work in the long run. Marriage is a matter of "we," not "me."

To get the best response, I encourage each of you to begin by outlining tentative plans for the next six months, one year, and five years separately. Now, don't pass out when you compare plans. That's just part of the process. Your mate will want different things than you, but together you may have a great plan. So get back together with your rough drafts, compare notes, and then commit to praying together over these matters. Ask God what He wants for you, and in light of the leading you get, revise your plans together.

Strive for excellence, not perfection. Share this chapter with your mate before you proceed.

Today my mate and I made a commitment to work on our plans for our future success and have a rough draft within one week.

_____   _____

YOUR SIGNATURE   DATE

CONCLUDING PRINCIPLE:

Failing to plan is planning to fail.

CHAPTER 13

THE HUSBAND-WIFE TEAM

If you are a married man, why should you listen to your wife, especially about business? Well, I can tell you, if you don't, you will probably live to regret it. It may be one of the hardest things you ever do, but a wise man will seek the counsel of his wife in his business matters.

I know in my own life, I can look back over the last forty years and see where things would be a lot different—for the better—if I had just listened to my wife's intuition more. I would have saved myself a tremendous amount of anxiety, pressure, and financial loss. Do you listen to your wife very well?

"I JUST HAD TO HAVE IT"

I remember the time I wanted to buy this particular piece of construction machinery. It was one of the finest pieces of equipment I had ever seen. I made arrangements to purchase it for $130,000. I was so excited, I could hardly sleep at night. It was massive, with the capacity to lift seventy-five tons. I still get excited when I think about it.

I took some photographs of it and took them home to show my wife, Janet, thinking she would be equally impressed. As I told her all about it, she listened intently. She didn't say a word. And when I finished with my burst of enthusiasm, I could tell she wasn't impressed. In fact, when it was her turn to talk, she only asked one question. "Van, what are you going to do with it?"

She might as well have slapped me in the face. In all honesty, I didn't have a clue. Actually, I knew some things I could use a crane for, but to say I could justify spending $130,000 on a piece of machinery was impossible. The truth was I just wanted to own that crane.

I was too embarrassed to answer her question truthfully, so I did what most men do. I responded to her question by saying, "Well, that just shows how little you know about construction. I'm not even going to answer that stupid question!"

I used to think that the best defense with my wife was a good offense. But God put my wife in my life as a helpmate, and it took me the better part of forty years to really let her start helping me. The history of my marriage has been getting Janet's counsel after the fact. I'd make up my mind on a matter first, and it was always "the ultimate deal." I was going to make a fortune. It was going to be fun and we would finally see our lifetime dreams fulfilled.

You know, I've done that more than twenty times in my life. That's how many new businesses I've owned. Janet had some serious reservations about most of them. She would say, "Well, I don't think you ought to do this," or, "Why did you do that?" "You shouldn't borrow that kind of money," or, "I don't feel good about that," "Why are you selling this?" or, "Why are you buying that?" Sometimes I resented her questions because they had so much common sense in them.

I just wanted to do my own thing and felt like she was sort of along for the ride. As a matter of fact, she was in the boat with me. If the boat sank, she sank. She didn't have a choice in the matter. If I cut a hole in the bottom of the boat, she was a goner. And if she tried to stop me, I wouldn't listen to her. I didn't want to listen to her. I felt like her questions were an attack on my masculinity or leadership or authority in the family.

Do you listen to your wife? I tell you what, God has been teaching me something grand about love and faithfulness through my wife. I've closed her out of many decisions. She's been hurt and cut off, and yet she has stuck by me. Now that's love. That's commitment. Would you continue to support your spouse if she made radical decisions without your agreement, especially when you could see how dumb those decisions were? Would you stick with a sinking ship? Maybe God is trying to show you what a great spouse you really have through all the circumstances you're facing today.

It has taken many years, but I've learned the wisdom of seeking my wife's counsel. I've not only seen this in my life, but in the lives of hundreds of couples I have counseled. Hundreds and hundreds of men have learned the same thing I have. They all say the same thing: "If only I had listened to my wife, I wouldn't be in this trouble."

There's a biblical reason that undergirds this experience. God designed your marriage to be a team effort between you and your wife. Here's what God says about His plan for marriage: "For this cause a man shall leave his father and his mother, and shall cleave to his wife; and they shall become one flesh" (Genesis 2:24).

How can you be one flesh if you leave her out of such a large portion of your life? How can you agree on a matter if you don't even tell her what you're doing? If she disagrees with your plan, you need to straighten out the problem. Find out why she disagrees and work through the issue until you both are at peace.

Including your wife in your decision making does-n't mean that you are taking commands from her. That's not what I'm talking about. Think of her as the radar system built into your marriage. When she senses danger or threat, listen to her. If she has suggestions or input, consider her wise counsel and the perspective she represents. When you include her, she will be better prepared (and so will you) to weather the storms that can arise. If she understands what's going on in your life, she'll be able to minister to you better, and to love and take care of you more.

Sometimes we get so wrapped up in what we're doing that we just don't want to include our wives. We want the credit. We want to be macho and be in control or make our wives think we're extra smart. We try to build up some kind of image to make others see how important we are or how independent and strong we are. We don't want to ask anyone for help.

After forty years of business experience, I've learned that it's not smart to leave my wife out of the picture. It makes about as much sense as trying to pad-dle a boat with one oar in the water. You may think you're going somewhere, but when you look back over a lifetime, you're just spinning in circles. God puts the priority of marriage over work. He designed your wife as a helpmate to your life, and you're missing out if you think that only means washing dishes, fixing supper, washing clothes, and changing dirty diapers.

GOD DESIGNED WIVES
TO HELP, NOT HINDER!

God created wives with a different set of operating tools than we have. It has been proven scientifically that women have different characteristics in their brains. They have intuition, and usually men don't have much of that. Women sense things men don't see.

And God will work through your wife to regain your attention. You know how men are. It's easy to get caught up in a project and just stop listening to God. Or maybe you want just a "little clearance" from God or a little direction from Him, and you think, *I can handle it from here.* And you run off and leave God in the dust. Is that the way you're living right now? As I'll discuss in chapter 16, men who run ahead of God usually have to report to the end of the line. You may not have to keep showing up at the end of the line if you decide to listen to what your wife says. I've heard Larry Burkett, the president of Christian Financial Concepts, say many times that when a man stops listening to God, He just goes over to the man's wife and says, "Go tell that dummy what I'm trying to tell him." God will speak through your wife if you cut Him off.

It always amazes me the way men will take my advice for their businesses even though I am a complete stranger. They've never seen me before in their lives, but they come to my office, and I spend sixteen or eighteen hours with them, evaluating a business that they've been in for years and years. I do some analysis and tell them what I think they need to do. And they listen. They make changes—big changes like buying and selling, or completely refocusing their marketing efforts—based on what I tell them. They take my advice, even though I am a perfect stranger, and I may not ever see them again in their lives.

Yet, these same men close out the advice of their wives who loved them enough to marry them, live with them, and put up with their mistakes. These faithful wives bear and raise their children (often nearly alone), cook for them, wash their clothes, and love them in spite of their messes. Yet somehow the husbands will not listen to a word from their wives. Instead, they act like they have something to prove by ignoring the suggestions or input from their wives.

I can say that because I used to be a husband like that. Ego is not that big of a deal to me now, I don't think. But it could be. Is it with you? Are you willing to continue suffering all the losses and business beatings you're taking just because you're too proud to listen to someone who loves you very much—your wife? How smart is that, really?

HE SHOULD HAVE LISTENED SOONER

I remember one particular couple from Virginia that I counseled who had owned their business for quite a number of years. Their three children were adults, had graduated from college, married, and settled in nearby states with their families. The wife was obviously having a difficult time with her children not only out of the nest, but out of state as well. And she adored her grandchildren.

The husband was more wrapped up in the business. Due to some changing economic factors, he started getting into some serious problems. Failing to see and make the necessary adjustments, the business nose-dived even more.

All along, his wife told him that things were not going to get any better, and that they needed to sell out and move closer to where the children lived. Well, he would have no part of that. Figuring that selling the business was just a ploy on her part to move closer to the children and grandchildren, the man resisted her counsel. He bristled at the thought of being manipulated by her, so the business continued to suffer month after month of losses. Yet he still would not listen.

I admire the wife. She continued to pray for him, submit to him, and truly love him in spite of her broken heart. She was losing everything, having neither time with her family nor prosperity in the business. Having no other options, she waited on God to move in her husband's heart and mind.

And He did. God allowed the inevitable to happen. The man lost both the business and their home. They lost their furniture, bank accounts, cars, everything. And she lost everything he lost, even though the disaster could have been averted if he just would have listened.

When I met these two, they were very, very discouraged. You can imagine how the husband felt—about as low as someone can get. Like Frank Sinatra sang, he was determined to do it "his way," and he lost everything they had worked for.

I believe God gave this man's wife a special measure of grace. He had to. She was such a precious person. She didn't nag, or say I told you so, or kick her husband when he was down. Neither did she mention moving to be closer to the children anymore. She just kept loving him and praying for him and encouraging him all the more.

And when the man was completely broken, God got his attention through his wife. He eventually concluded how wise it would be to move closer to his children and start a new business. Since then, I understand they have made that move and are doing very well. Just think of all the agony this man could have been spared if he had listened to his wife's wisdom earlier.

How well do you listen to your wife? God gave her to you as a helpmate, but do you let her help? Try thinking through what she says. You may not understand why she says what she does, and that's OK. Neither does she have to be a business expert. What matters is that she loves the Lord, that she listens to Him, and that she's really committed to what's best for you. If you have a wife like that, you'd be wise to tune in to her.

TRY THIS TO IMPROVE
YOUR LISTENING SKILLS

Below are two methods you could try to improve your listening skills with your wife. They have worked for me and for others, and they might be just what you need to get going.

Ask for her advice, but include this statement: "What I would like you to do is tell me how you feel about . . . ," and then tell her whatever subject you want to talk about and get her counsel on. Next, either record her answers or make notes. Doing so will show her that you're genuinely interested in what she has to say.

I think it's helpful to let her know that you are not going to make any comments or respond in any way other than asking more questions for the next twenty-four hours. She'll respond to you more candidly and completely if she knows you're not going to jump her case at every point she makes. If you start shouting or become hostile, angry, or defensive about everything she says, you'll cut her off.

After she has finished, take her answers and pray. Let God help you to clearly see what your wife is saying, and ask God to help you understand both her counsel and His will in this matter. And be sure to give her positive feedback on her insights so she will know you really heard her. Tell her, "You know, I've thought and prayed about what you said last night, and I believe you're right on target. I just never saw it that way before! I'm so glad you told me what was on your mind." If you do this, I promise that you'll not only gain new insights into your business decisions, but you'll be building a fantastic marriage as well.

This doesn't mean you'll agree on everything she says. You probably won't. But at least you've included her and sought God's counsel in light of what your helpmate has to say. And then, after twenty-four hours have passed, you can go back to her and say something like this: "Honey, it bothers me that we don't agree on this. Why don't we seek outside advice on this and see if we can come to a clearer understanding of how God is leading us? What do you think about talking to our pastor or somebody at the bank?" Taking action like this demonstrates that you really are listening to her and that you value her advice.

A second method is to take turns talking rather than taking notes and waiting for a day to pass. Give your wife thirty minutes to talk without interruption, and then you take thirty minutes. If you like, you can take notes. When you have finished, review what you heard the other person saying, and then seek out God's will for you in prayer *together*.

MAKING MARRIAGE A TEAM EFFORT

The goal is to open the lines of communication between the two of you and the Lord. Even if she doesn't agree with you, she'll know what's going on in your heart. And since she'll know what you're planning to do, she'll have a minimum number of unexpected surprises to cope with. I've talked to dozens and dozens of wives who discovered that their husbands were in serious financial trouble only when the sheriff came and repossessed their cars or when they were evicted from their homes. You'd be upset too if your spouse had risked all your life savings or your home without your knowledge. That's not too hard to understand. No wonder so many spouses get upset. And when your spouse loses that core sense of trust in you, it creates a deep wound that takes a long time to heal.

When God created your marriage to be a team effort, He didn't say that you're only a team when you're at home, playing a game, or on vacation. He meant you're a team with your business and career as well. What you do has a tremendous impact on everyone else in your family. You are to be "one" and function as "one."

If you're not including your wife by seeking her counsel, it's time for you to start. Talk things over with her. If you've never done it this way, you may have to swallow your pride to get started. That's OK because God never said He would defend your pride. In fact, it's likely that your pride is standing in the way of what He's trying to do in your life. Opening the communication lines to your wife may not be easy, but the rewards will be great if you'll simply listen to her and heed her counsel. You may still disagree with her, but at least you've taken the time to listen to her heart. You've included her as part of the team, and doing so may save your marriage when times get tough.

Make a commitment, not only to listen to your wife, but to take action on at least some aspect of her counsel. If she thinks you're just listening to be polite, it will discourage her from being honest with you in the future. After all, a woman who sees her good suggestions to her husband being ignored will not speak up readily. Try one of the methods I've listed above. If you know a better idea, use it. The goal is to open communications between you and your wife in a way that God can bless and in which He can be glorified. And I promise you, He will be glorified when He sees you working together in His power and Spirit, and on your knees together seeking His will. Now that's a fantastic marriage!

Make the commitment today to seek your wife's counsel and act on it. You can begin by showing her this chapter and asking her if she agrees. Just have your pencil and notepad ready. When the two of you work together, God can not only lift you out of the bottom of the barrel. He can raise you up as a witness to your children, your neighbors, and even to the uttermost parts of the world. And you'll be witnessing to God's power in your lives . . . together. Won't it be great to be friends working as a unit again, instead of fighting against each other as enemies?

I commit myself to seeking my spouse's counsel for me in every area of my life because I believe God has important insights for me to learn from my soulmate.

_____   _____

Your signature   Date

CONCLUDING PRINCIPLE:

Unless two are agreed, how can they walk together?

SECTION THREE
LET'S
TAKE ACTION

CHAPTER 14

ARE YOU BEING TRANSPARENT?

"Who cares about being transparent, whatever that means? I've got problems. And I need a solution right now, not some nonsense about being transparent."

That is what I thought when someone first told me I needed to be transparent. I had more important things to do. I was in trouble, and I didn't have time for anything that wouldn't help me today. Hurting people want help right now. So let's look at the issue from a different angle: Are you being *honest* with those around you about the issues you're facing? Or are you presenting a facade that says, "Other people may have problems, but I don't"?

At first I resisted the idea myself. But then I discovered the strength that comes from being honest and transparent with others. By transparency, I mean being open and aboveboard about what your needs are in such a way that others can help. For example, letting people know that you can't pay them now but you are working on a way to pay them. Let them know you will call or come and see them with a plan in a week, or whenever you can. Your greatest need of the moment may be learning to be honest with God, your wife, a business associate . . . or perhaps even yourself!

Being transparent is much like getting a shot in the arm. It hurts at the moment, but it is an important step to getting better. Being transparent with others about your needs may very well open the door to God's answer to the problems you're facing right now. What if God has supplied the answer to your need *right now* through someone else, but you won't receive that answer until the person is made aware of your need?

IT'S EASY TO HIDE THESE!

Men typically hide things from others, especially their wives. Just scan the list below and see if you habitually hide these areas from other people. You might be surprised to find you are hiding more than you thought.

- your failures
- your weaknesses
- your deep desire to be respected
- your fears
- your finances
- things you're guilty or ashamed of
- your relationship with Jesus Christ
- your emotional needs

You may be hiding other things I have not mentioned. You may not be ready to open up your soul to anyone just yet. That's OK. I just want you to know that you're not alone. Most of us hide things from others. And sometimes there are good reasons to hide.

Listen, when I just think about being open and transparent in every area of my life, I get uptight. I've got good reason to be private with some of my thoughts and feelings. If I'm going to tell anyone, it will be God.

Every area of your life is important to God, and opening up with Him in prayer takes real courage. Strong men stand openly before God. He already knows everything about you, including those deep, dark secrets.

There are also poor reasons to hide our real thoughts and needs from others. Check out the list below for reasons that you keep secrets from others.

☐ I'm afraid of what others will think.
☐ I don't understand my relationship to Jesus Christ.
☐ I am afraid of being exposed for who I really am.
☐ I'm unwilling to stop and repent of my sin.
☐ I'm too embarrassed by what I have done.
☐ I'm too proud.
☐ I have a poor relationship with my wife or children.
☐ I want to be a hero to my wife and children.
☐ The boss will fire me.
☐ I'm afraid I'll be taken advantage of.
☐ I will lose everyone's respect.
☐ I'm lonely and scared.

Did any of them fit? If not, you may be so used to calling them by different names that you missed them. Read the list again—slowly. In all my years of counseling, I can think of literally hundreds and hundreds of broken lives and marriages that could have been saved if the issues above could have been talked out. They simply needed to be faced, dealt with using God's principles, and dealt with immediately. Families could have been saved.

I know it's scary to let other people in on your troubles, especially if you've been burned before. I know what those feelings are like. But here's the truth. *You can run, but you really can't hide.* There are people in your life, especially your wife, who already know you pretty well. They probably know more about you than you think they do—or more than you really want them to know. And most wives still love their husbands and continue to live with them in spite of who they are and what they've done. That may be the case with your wife too.

I'll let you in on a little secret I learned. Most of the solutions I've offered to business men and women in financial chaos come from two sources: *God and their mate.*

When I counsel someone in trouble, I always ask the spouse to attend one of the early sessions. I have found that a wife usually has a very accurate under-standing of what is going on in her husband's life. Some call it intuition. I'm not sure what to call it; I just know wives have something like a God-given radar system that helps them to see through their husbands.

When the counseling session opens, I ask the hus-band to encourage his wife to give her insights into his problem and possible solutions. A wife usually can pin-point both her husband's problems and the necessary remedies. And she doesn't even have to understand business to know what her husband's real issues are.

SHE DIDN'T KNOW WHAT HE NEEDED

I recall working with a man who was in so much trouble that he had pulled back from all his business responsibilities except for selling. He completely ignored his twenty-four employees, phone calls from the IRS, and the demands of angry creditors. He even brushed aside unhappy customers. Like a horse with blinders, the man had one thing in mind: selling. Things finally got so bad that he called me in to help him.

I spent two days evaluating his situation, talking to his employees, and examining what little bookkeeping he had. At each step of the process, I prayed and asked God for insight and wisdom. In return, it became pretty obvious to me that this man was not qualified to run a business, and the sooner he got out, the better off he would be.

Prior to discussing his options, I met him and his wife for dinner. I was particularly interested in her insights into her husband and his business. And so, at the right time, I asked him if she could be candid with me about her thoughts on his business and how he ran it. He not only agreed, but he encouraged her to comment on everything in detail.

She began by sharing what a wonderful husband he was, how much she loved him, and how much it hurt her to see him struggle. Then came her key insight. She said that he was really good at sales and promotion, but he was not very good at running things. She went on to suggest that he would be happier working for someone else, rather than having responsibility for all the employees, paying bills, and collecting on accounts.

She proposed several fantastic ideas on how he could make the transition from being an employer to an employee. I was amazed at her insight, and I thought, *What am I doing here? They have all the answers between them.*

He was living with the right answer, his wife. But because he had never been transparent with her about the business, he lost more than $500,000. Acting on her insights, however, he got someone to take over the company. He now works as a district sales manager for one of his former suppliers. Get this. His salary and commissions for the first year totaled more than $75,000, twice as much as he had ever made in a year in his own business.

That's not the end of the story, however. He continued to open up to his wife and they really grew in their marriage. He couldn't wait to get home from work to be with her. And amazingly, her respect for her husband grew, not diminished, because of his willingness to be open. He said he never dreamed marriage could be so good.

I had to learn the hard way. I was reared to keep quiet about my needs. If I didn't open up, no one would know anything. Wrong thinking! If no one knew what my needs were, how could they possibly help? I've learned that God has called others into my life to help me, and for me to reciprocate by helping them. No man is an island. I'm not, and neither are you.

If you are a married man, God has truly brought your wife into your life as your helpmate. Talk to her. Let her know what's going on in your life. It may be rough at first. It may be frustrating to share when you start, but it is a good time to start learning to listen. In fact, God may be trying to get your attention through what she has to say.

I have heard literally hundreds of men say something like this, "If I had only listened to my wife I wouldn't be in this trouble."

Others have said, "I didn't tell her what I was doing until it was too late. I wanted to be a hero and show her that I could make it on my own. All along I should have been working *with* her as my partner rather than leaving her out.

Genesis 2:24 says, "They shall become one flesh." That means you're a team, a unit. What happens to one of you will necessarily impact the other. Don't fall into the trap of thinking that God's answer to your problem will always be revealed directly to you. It doesn't always happen that way. In fact, He may very well supply the answer to your needs through your spouse.

And maybe He will not only work through your spouse. God uses all kinds of people and situations to meet your real needs. He may raise up a friend, neighbor, business associate, or someone from your church. But you have to be willing to be transparent by letting people know who you are and what's happening in your life. After all, are you primarily a *businessman* in business, or a *Christian* in business? There's a lot of difference. I encourage you to let others know you're a believer in the Lord Jesus Christ. You may be pleasantly surprised at how quickly God can work in your life when others know you're a Christian.

Paul taught that Christians who have a surplus are to share with those who are enduring hard times. He told the Corinthians, "Our desire is not that others might be relieved while you are hard pressed, but that there might be equality. At the present time your plenty will supply what they need, so that in turn their plenty will supply what you need. Then there will be equality" (2 Corinthians 8:13–14 NIV).

The temptation is to be open about the good things and hide the failures. Listen. Your greatest disasters may be the occasion for God's greatest miracles to be worked. Look at what the apostle Paul says in 2 Corinthians

12:9— "And He has said to me, 'My grace is sufficient for you, for power is perfected in weakness.' Most gladly, therefore, I will rather boast about my weaknesses, so that the power of Christ may dwell in me."

I know this from personal experience. When I'm at the bottom of the barrel, I'm closer to God than I ever am when everything is going well. I have to depend on Him. And I get encouragement by having strong believers surround me. Sometimes I have to lean on their strong faith when mine is weak. The key for me is to be transparent with God and others. Doing so opens the door wide for help.

I remember a man named Bill who had a wife and four children. What he *didn't* have was a job, or even transportation to get him to a job. One Sunday morning, while worshiping with his church family, he prayed out loud during the morning prayer time, asking God to help him with both a job and transportation. An attorney sitting two pews in front of him heard the prayer, and God put it on his heart to help Bill with a car. The attorney had two cars, one a fixer-upper, and the other was . . . well, much nicer. You and I would be glad to have it. Guess which car the Lord put on the attorney's heart to give? You're right, the nicer one. That's just the way the Lord works.

STEPS TO BECOMING
TRANSPARENT WITH OTHERS

Here are some steps to follow that will help you grow in being transparent with others.

Be open with the Lord. He knows what you need, but it will help you to confess what is happening in your life to the Lord anyway. And when I say everything, I mean *everything*. Talk to Him every day. Keeping a close relationship with Jesus Christ is the single most important thing you can do to get on top again. God is on your side. He wants you to be a success and a winner. Open up to Him and let Him do "His thing."

Talk to your spouse every day, if possible. If you are a married man, you need to make communication with your wife a high priority. Not just "hi, how ya doing?" but tell her what's on your heart. Discuss where the two of you are financially. Tell her some of your fears. Let her know what you're thinking about doing and ask for her input. Keep her posted when the good and bad happen. You may be surprised how much insight God gives women. Start today. Take her on a date and let her into your life.

Take a chance. Everyone I have ever known or read about has failed (except for Jesus Christ), most more than once. I read that Bill Gates, the president and founder of Microsoft, will not hire anyone for a management position unless the person has previously failed. His reason? If a man hasn't failed, he hasn't taken any chances, and a man who doesn't take chances can't be on the cutting edge.

Get out of your comfort zone. With God in you and around you, you can't lose. You have to be willing to step out in faith with people and situations. Tell people about your faith in Jesus Christ and how you trust Him in every situation. Try to tell someone about Jesus every day. Sure, you'll be rejected by some, maybe many. But guess what? People also rejected Jesus.

Determine why you are doing what you are doing. Are you really hiding from the issues? Are you fooling yourself? Go back to the list early in this chapter and see which reasons for hiding match up with you. Write them down and talk to your spouse about them. Ask someone to hold you accountable for facing your problems head-on and seeking help from others.

BENEFITS OF BEING TRANSPARENT

Here are the benefits you will reap if you pursue this step of becoming transparent with others.

By being transparent, you will transfer the responsibility for the outcome to God. When you do it God's way, the outcome is in His hands . . . no more running, hiding, fearing people or situations. People will begin to respect you for your boldness. I've seen wonderful things happen when people in serious trouble reached out to help someone else. People were looking at them to learn why. *Who would do such a thing?* they wondered.

By being transparent, you give God an opportunity to meet your needs. When you are hiding, how can God bring someone else into your life to help? If you hide from Him, how can He work through you?

Being transparent will help to keep you out of trouble. When you commit to openness and honesty with others, your actions will no longer be secret. Exposure stops many a sin.

Make the commitment today to become the godly, transparent man or woman your Father in heaven wants you to be. You can do it. To be sure, you will be living on the edge, but the edge is a great place to be when Jesus is there.

And my God will supply all your needs according to His riches in glory in Christ Jesus. (Philippians 4:19)

Today, _____/_____/_____, *I made the commitment
to become the transparent person God wants me to be.*

_____   _____

YOUR SIGNATURE   DATE

I have told

_____

about this commitment.

CONCLUDING PRINCIPLE:

*Being transparent
allows God to
work in your life.*

CHAPTER 15
DEALING WITH CREDITORS

What would you think if you sold something to a person who failed to pay you? What if you were unable to pay *your* bills because this same person had failed to pay? I don't know about you, but I'd be pretty upset.

To further complicate the picture, what if this person failed to return your phone calls and was never around when you went to his office? What if he completely avoided you, leaving you without a clue as to if and when he ever planned to pay you?

I'd be pretty angry, and I expect you would be too. Your creditors are people, also, and their reaction is probably no different than yours would be if someone owed you money. The truth is that you are complicating their business operations if you're unable to pay your bills on time. In this chapter I'm going to give you some practical steps to follow to improve your relationship with your creditors, tell you how to deal with the IRS, and suggest a plan to know whom to pay and when.

DON'T AVOID YOUR CREDITORS

One of the biggest mistakes I see people make is avoiding creditors because they lack the money to pay them. My advice is don't avoid your creditors; instead, do everything you can to work with them. They have a genuine interest in your business, because most realize the sooner you get back on your feet financially, the sooner they'll get paid.

However, you will find some creditors who will not be satisfied by anything less than your cash in their hands, so brace yourself. They may be angry toward you regardless of what you do and how humble your attitude is. Accept that, and resolve to treat them as Jesus would, remembering that the Son of God loved His adversaries even when they abused Him.

Surprisingly, it is usually the smaller creditors, those you owe $300–$500, that will give you the most trouble. The larger creditors, generally speaking, will not become upset if you just work out a plan to pay them back and stick to it.

Keep in mind that your goal as a believer should be to rebuild a trust relationship with your creditors. To help you, I've listed some specific steps for you to follow. If you stick to these actions, you'll be making the best of a bad situation.

1. PRAY FOR YOUR CREDITORS BY NAME

I'm not talking about some spiritually polite prayer for your problem. I mean the real thing. Ask the Holy Spirit to intervene in their hearts, bringing an abundance of wisdom, grace, and forgiveness. Ask the Holy Spirit to go before you prior to each encounter you have with them, and ask Him to defuse any fleshly, sinful attitudes they are harboring against you. Most of all, ask the Holy Spirit to provide a witness for you in the midst of these painful, unusual circumstances.

Don't overlook the ministry of the Holy Spirit at this critical stage in your life by failing to pray for His intervention with your creditors.

2. Take the Initiative to Contact Your Creditors

Don't wait for them to call you. Instead, seek them out, and, if possible, meet with them face to face. Doing so will make you more credible. When you meet, simply explain what your predicament is. Businesses get into trouble for a lot of reasons, so level with your creditors about your situation. Don't be defensive about it either. State your intention to follow biblical principles of repaying what you owe, no matter how long it takes. When you tie your motives to biblical roots, God will begin to open a door for you to witness.

Does the Bible really indicate that debtors need to pay even debts that can be legally canceled? "The wicked borrows and does not pay back, but the righteous is gracious and gives" (Psalm 37:21).

3. Develop a Plan to Repay Creditors

Sit down and make a list of every person you owe along with the amount. Develop your plan to repay by negotiating with each creditor to discover how flexible they can be with you.

You may want to begin paying off the smaller debts first, followed by attacking the larger ones. Your plan should address the amounts due to each creditor, when you intend to begin repaying them, the amount of each payment, and the length of time you expect to take. Get each creditor to agree to your proposal. And if you need to make changes along the way, let your creditors know as soon as you realize that the changes must be made.

I worked with a man named Michael who proposed a plan to his creditors and managed to repay everyone. He owned a specialty packaging company that had sales of over $1 million per year. One year, through no fault of his own, he ended up with a negative net worth of $300,000. When he realized what had happened, Michael immediately devised a plan to keep the company afloat.

His plan included selling one of the two family cars (the better one) and his home, putting the proceeds back into the business. He went to his banker and negotiated a plan to pay only one-half of his interest for the next two years, followed by paying interest only for the five years after that, and then a resumption of both principal and interest payments. Because Michael had a comprehensive plan, the banker agreed.

Michael leveled with all the employees at his company, stating his desire to save the company (and their jobs!). Rather than cutting salaries or laying people off, he sought the cooperation of the entire workforce in working hard, being efficient, and doing everything they could do to maximize the company's profit margin.

He then drafted a revised budget and took the entire plan to his creditors, whom he contacted individually. Of the twenty-three creditors, only three small ones were difficult. Michael provided each creditor with a complete list of whom he owed money to, how much he owed, and a projected schedule for repayment that would take up to eight years for some.

Predictably, some of the small creditors were upset and were unwilling to wait for up to eight years for repayment. So Michael talked to the larger creditors and came to an agreement to pay off the smaller ones first. In the end, everyone agreed.

Most creditors will respect a person's honest intentions to pay them off. Having a plan will not only help you to bring organization to chaos, but it may also open doors to negotiate possibilities that you otherwise wouldn't have.

4. TELL THE TRUTH ABOUT YOUR ENTIRE FINANCIAL SITUATION

Let everyone know what you owe to all your creditors. Just lay it all out. If some of them force you into bankruptcy, they'll all find out what your situation is anyway. Being honest will help most creditors to see that you're sincere and really do want to repay them.

One man I worked with did just the opposite and lost his credibility and his witness for Christ. He owned a fireplace shop and installed inserts into new homes. Unknowingly, he was losing money month after month. When he realized how bad his problem was, however, he placed a large order for fireplaces and supplies and sold them all at cut prices. With all the cash in hand, he told his wife that he had sold the fireplace store and that he intended to take her on a vacation, followed by a change of residence to another city. *The man simply lied and walked away from his debt.*

Much to his surprise, his creditors tracked him down and began filing lawsuits and attaching things.

His reputation as a businessman and a Christian was completely destroyed. Not only had he lied to his creditors, but he lied to his wife, who ultimately divorced him. All relationships, including your marriage and your relationship with creditors, must be built on trust. Trust builds alongside your reputation for telling the truth, no matter what.

5. STICK TO YOUR PLAN UNTIL EVERYONE IS REPAID

I remember my father telling me this story from back in the Depression days. At the time, he was making $12 for working a sixty-hour week. One of his co-workers asked to borrow a dollar from him, saying he would repay it the following Saturday. About ten o'clock the following Saturday night, there was a knock at the door. The co-worker had walked two miles in pouring rain to keep his commitment to repay.

People used to be like that. Paying back a debt was normal—people couldn't even imagine anything else. If they ran into a problem repaying what they owed, they'd come to tell you about it. Today such honesty is almost unheard of, even among Christians.

You can have a tremendous impact for the sake of Christ just by striving to keep your word and repay what you owe. Get your plan together and stick to it until you pay everyone what you owe them. Do it for the sake of Jesus Christ.

DEALING WITH THE IRS

You probably cringed when you read that title because employees of the IRS have a reputation for being some of the worst people on earth to work with. Even if they are difficult, they're still people whom

Christ died for and, as such, they deserve love and respect. Generally I have found that the IRS will work with you fairly if you work fairly with them. Of course there are exceptions.

If you owe back taxes, contact the IRS and seek a settlement. I know one man who owed more than $125,000 in back taxes. He worked out an offer with the IRS and settled for $1,600.

IF BANKRUPTCY IS YOUR ONLY OPTION

Filing for bankruptcy should be seen as a "last resort" rather than your first choice. However, bankruptcy is not the end of the world. You can survive, sustain your Christian witness, and ultimately recover from bankruptcy with God's help. Indeed, there may be times when it is appropriate to file for bankruptcy. The key is the motive of your heart.

If you're filing simply to avoid paying back what you owe others, don't expect God to bless that choice. God specifically addresses that motive in the following passage: "When you make a vow to God, do not be late in paying it, for He takes no delight in fools. Pay what you vow! It is better that you should not vow than you should vow and not pay" (Ecclesiastes 5:4–5).

THOUGHTS ON FILING FOR BANKRUPTCY

I believe you should make every attempt to avoid filing for bankruptcy. However, you may have already filed. Or you may be in the process of filing or being forced into bankruptcy against your will, illustrating the truth of Proverbs 22:7. The following situations may lead you to consider filing for bankruptcy.

1. If you're concerned about your mental health or that of your spouse, bankruptcy may be a prudent option to relieve the financial pressure temporarily. Some people are pushed to suicidal thoughts as a result of financial mistakes and the resulting pressure to pay what is owed. Bankruptcy may be a step to protecting the health and well-being of your family for the short term.

2. If one of your creditors is taking all your assets to the exclusion of all other creditors, filing for bankruptcy may ensure a more equitable distribution of your remaining assets.

3. You may not have a choice. Three or more of your creditors can put you into bankruptcy whether you want it or not.

4. If your creditors put pressure on you to break laws or participate in illegal activities, bankruptcy may be a step toward protecting your integrity and Christian witness.

Bankruptcy for a Christian is an option only for the purpose of giving you a way to pay back your creditors. Psalm 37:21 clearly states that it is your responsibility to repay. Even though human courts may absolve you of all responsibility, they do not supersede God's truth.

It may seem impossible at this moment to ever pay everyone back, but nothing is impossible with God. He has the resources, but you must have the willing heart. Regardless of your reason for filing bankruptcy, you can maintain your dignity, honor, and Christian witness through a commitment to repay all of your debts in full.

The good news is, once you make that firm commitment, God will come to your side, bless your faith, and begin to supply resources to you that you've never dreamed of. When you combine your faith with obedience to God's Word, some amazing things can happen. Indeed, God is still alive and works miracles today.

Would you make a commitment now? Would you commit to dealing with your creditors in a way that will reflect the Lord Jesus Christ? Commit to working with them openly and honestly and in a way that would honor Jesus. If you would do that, please sign your name below and date it.

_____   _____

YOUR SIGNATURE   DATE

CONCLUDING PRINCIPLE:

*A vow given is
a vow to keep.*

CHAPTER 16

NO TIME TO WAIT

*A*re you scared with no time to waste? I know you don't feel like you have time to wait for anything. I know the pressure you're under when the IRS attaches your bank account. I know how helpless you feel when served an eviction notice or when your car is repossessed or a thousand other things go wrong. I know about being scared with no time to waste.

MARTY JUST COULDN'T WAIT

You feel like you must do something today even if it's wrong. You may feel like one person I talked to. Let me tell you about Marty. *She was too busy to wait.*

Marty was a registered pharmacist who had inherited her father's drugstore. It had been on the same downtown corner for fifty-six years. She was the only support for her mother and her sister, who had been retarded since birth. The store had been losing money since the big discount stores had opened on the edge of town. As Marty's losses mounted and the inventory went down, she grew angry with God. How could He let this happen to her when she had been so faithful all these years, taking care of her family, teaching Sunday school, and giving her life for others? Now she would end up with nothing. The other merchants on her block had sold their empty buildings for whatever they could get.

Her mother had begged her to talk to her pastor or some godly person about what to do. Her mother quoted Psalm 27:14 to her: "Wait for the Lord; be strong and let your heart take courage; yes, wait for the Lord." God had never let them down and He would not start now, she said. Marty responded sarcastically by saying that if God wanted to help, the store would still be open, or at least He would have sent a buyer who would pay enough for them to live on.

When Marty finally decided to close her doors, a local man offered to buy her building for $25,000 if she would sign the contract within seven days.

She couldn't believe the low price. She had spent that much to remodel the store five years ago. After checking around, she discovered that not only was that the best offer; it was the *only* offer she could get. Marty signed the papers and took the money. She even muttered under her breath, "*Thanks a lot, God.*" Marty was so angry with God that she quit having quiet times. She didn't want to listen to Him because, in her mind, He had failed her completely.

Six months later a national bank bought the entire block to build a computer center, and Marty's old drugstore was the key piece of property. The bank was willing to pay more than $200,000 for it. God had already made plans to take care of Marty's whole family. If only she had waited on Him.

"Morning by morning, O Lord, you hear my voice; morning by morning I lay my requests before you and wait in expectation" (Psalm 5:3 NIV).

IF ONLY I'D WAITED

"If only" have been the closing words of many tragic stories. When we fail to wait on the Lord, we are stopping God from giving His best to us. We cut off His plans. We stop Him short. If we go around God, He won't force us to take His way. He will let us "do it our way." But our plans fall miserably short of all that He has in store for us.

Is that your trouble? Have you been so anxious to get out of trouble that you have refused to seek wise counsel or even to listen to it when it was offered? Have you failed to stop and see what God is doing in your life? Do you wait for a clear direction from God before you act?

Listen and learn from my mistakes! There are so many times I have said to God, "I am going to do something and if You don't want me to do it, shut the door." How dumb can I be? You know the results of that kind of thinking, don't you? In my mind, God will be responsible if my plan fails, amounting to shifting the blame to God for my foolishness.

God may have already taken care of your problem. I cannot begin to tell you how many times I have said or heard other people say, "If only I had waited."

Don't get me wrong. There's a time to wait and a time to take action. No one expects you to sit around watching TV or being lazy under the guise of waiting on the Lord. Do what you can do without getting out of His will. If you can get a job cutting grass until God gives you clear direction, do it. You may be scared to do anything because everything has gone wrong. I understand that, but you can start with some small things and work up.

When you wait on the Lord for direction, you not only lessen the chances of making your situation worse; you will gain wisdom by seeing things from God's perspective.

WANTED: FINER THINGS NOW

Fred, a committed Christian, had struggled with his small, five-employee plumbing company for more than seven years, and he still was not making the money he thought he deserved. He worked long hours and had a great reputation for quality. The business was doing well, but Fred wanted more of the finer things in life. He lived in a small community, which was better for his children, but Fred wanted "the big times." After talking to several friends and two deacons from his church about what he should do, he heard the same message: "Fred, be patient and wait on the Lord." He even went so far as to ask his wife, and she agreed with the others.

About this time, Fred heard through a local fast food manager that the home office would be taking bids in thirty days to supply all the plumbing maintenance for the forty-three stores in his area. They would even make a minimum monthly payment. If he could just land that contract, he thought, he would be able to reach his goals quickly.

The problem was that there were seventeen other bidders on the project. Fred didn't believe he had a chance, but he talked to the Lord anyway and asked God for the contract. When the award date passed and he didn't hear anything from the company, he knew the contract had been given to someone else. Fred started making plans to close down his business and go to work for a larger company in another city. At the new job, he could make a lot more money and he wouldn't have to wait on the things he had always wanted.

Fred's wife pleaded for him to wait on the Lord. She reminded him that God's ways were not their ways, and that they were to walk by faith in God, and not by what they could see at the moment.

Fred didn't listen. He was too greedy. After interviewing with the owner of the large plumbing company, Fred agreed to supervise a crew for them.

Four months after he had closed his company and started the new job, Fred's wife got a call from the local fast food manager. The plumbing contractor who had been awarded the contract had defaulted. They were trying to find Fred so he could take over the work that very day. Fred could almost name his price. They checked on all the bidders and found that Fred's reputation was so good that he was their next choice.

But for Fred, it was too late. He had no men and no equipment. God had answered his prayer no doubt, but His time was not Fred's time. Because of his greed, the chance of a lifetime was gone.

We "get in a big hurry to get behind" when we don't wait on the Lord. As I look back over my life and see the times I failed to wait on the Lord, I am ashamed and embarrassed by what could have been if I had only not been in such a big hurry. If only I had waited and listened to the Lord!

IF YOU WAIT, YOU WILL GET AHEAD

Waiting on the Lord will get you ahead in life, not behind. I know that sounds like a contradiction, but let me show you what I mean.

A church had outgrown its facilities to the point that it was having three services on Sunday and two on Saturday night in order to seat the crowds. Something had to be done before it overworked its pastor to death. The church debated two positions: borrowing the money to build a new sanctuary or trusting God to supply all the funds before starting construction. The church already had the property because someone had given twelve acres when the church first started twenty-one years ago.

The pastor and elders finally decided that the Lord had led them to wait on Him, even though it would mean a tough schedule for the pastor. The real issue, they felt, was whether they trusted God or not. And the elders felt that it was better to wait on the Lord even if that meant never building a new church building. With just two exceptions, the congregation agreed.

A year passed, and it looked as though the Lord was not going to answer their prayers. Yet the people held firm in their faith, claiming the promise of Psalm 38:15—"For I hope in You, O Lord; You will answer, O Lord my God."

One year, eight months, and nine days after the decision to wait on the Lord, a man asked the pastor if the church would consider selling the property. He told the pastor how much his company was willing to pay for the twelve acres. Remarkably, it was enough to buy five acres at a better location and build a church facility larger than they had requested from the Lord.

"Trust in the Lord with all your heart and do not lean on your own understanding. In all your ways acknowledge Him, and He will make your paths straight" (Proverbs 3:5–6).

God made their pathways straight and supplied all they needed and more. Notice that God could not have done that if they had borrowed the money and built where they were. Borrowing would have bypassed His will for them.

HOW TO WAIT WHEN YOU'RE IN A HURRY

I'm assuming that you have taken care of all the things we have talked about in previous chapters. Doing so is a step of waiting on the Lord, because you're considering His thoughts and principles before acting. Below are listed some steps to follow when you're most tempted to run ahead of the Lord.

1. *Make a total commitment to wait on the Lord.* I'm not talking about lip service. I'm talking about the kind of commitment that says, "I will not take another step until I have a clear direction from God," rather than listening to feelings or seeing if it seems the right thing to do. Don't play with this. This is your life. You are the one who will stop losing and start winning. The most important part will be that you will be doing it God's way.

2. *While you're waiting on God, intensify your spiritual disciplines in order to clarify His will for you.* Make specific requests of God and keep a journal of His leading (see Jeremiah 33:3; Matthew 7:7; and James 1:5–8). Search the Bible for passages that address your situation (see Psalm 119:105; 2 Timothy 3:16–17).

3. *Talk to others;* God has placed many people in your life to help you avoid problems. Use them. Don't think you have to have all the answers yourself. Instead, seek the advice of godly individuals (see Psalm

1:1; Proverbs 11:14; and Proverbs 27:17). What seems obvious to you may look like a trap to someone else. Listen to godly counsel.

4. *Don't be pressured.* If you don't have complete peace about your next move, wait. Don't proceed until you do. If someone insists that you make a quick decision, look out. When you don't have time to pray and meditate about God's will in a decision, or even talk to your wife, then that's something you should let pass.

TATE JUST COULDN'T GET
PEACE ABOUT LEAVING

Let me finish this chapter with a quick story about someone who received poor counsel from everyone except the Lord, and chose to wait.

Tate had worked for the same man for twenty-two years and had peaked out in his career several years before. The work environment was great, but he still worked for someone else. He wanted to do something to have more authority, responsibility, and income. He was capable of running the company, but it was obvious the owner was going to be there forever.

Tate had been praying about what to do for more than a year but could not get peace about leaving. He had been offered a partnership in a competitor's company along with several job opportunities that paid more than what he was making.

Tate discussed these decisions with his wife, but she did not have a clear direction on what he should do. Several friends as well as his pastor encouraged him to make a move. From their point of view, he was stuck and could not go anywhere. After all, he was doing most of the work.

In the absence of God's clear leading, Tate continued to pray and wait on God. He had made a commitment not to leave his current job until he experienced
God's peace about making a change. He continued to
work as unto the Lord, doing the very best he knew
how. One day, almost three years after Tate had first
talked to the Lord about the future of his work, the
owner of the business died.

Tate was shocked, but not nearly so shocked as
when the attorney called to tell him that the owner had
left the company to him. Not one word had ever been
mentioned about Tate's being in the owner's will. Since
the owner didn't have any survivors, Tate got it all. God
had answered his prayers long before he inherited the
business, way back when Tate first made a commitment to wait on the Lord, no matter what.

Are you ready to make that commitment to wait on
the Lord, no matter what? Are you ready to give God
the freedom to answer your prayers? I heard a man say
one time, "I'll never know if God will perform a miracle
unless I give Him a chance."

"Wait for the Lord and keep His way, and He will
exalt you to inherit the land; when the wicked are cut
off, you will see it" (Psalm 37:34).

Are you ready? Let's do it now.

*I made a commitment to the Lord today to wait on Him
to show me what I'm supposed to do so I can do it.*

DATE _____ / _____ / _____

SIGNED

_____

I shared this commitment with the following people:

_____

_____

_____

_____

CONCLUDING PRINCIPLE:

> *People who get*
> *ahead of God*
> *usually have to go*
> *to the end of the line.*

CHAPTER 17

IS SOMEONE ELSE HURTING?

God had an interesting way of pulling Bill out of his depression, and the method might be exactly what you need. You might be surprised, however, to learn just exactly what that method involved.

I had counseled Bill for better than six months following the loss of his company, helping him to work through a deep depression. But nothing I tried could break the vise-like grip that depression held on him.

One day I asked Bill out to lunch. After we were seated in the restaurant, a mutual friend, Alton, walked in, and we asked him to join us. While we waited for our food, Alton told us that he had just been forced into bankruptcy by his creditors the previous week. For more than an hour, he poured out his heart to us, telling of vicious things that had been said and done. Alton was at the bottom of the barrel and he not only lacked hope; he even lacked *the energy* to hope.

You may recognize that feeling of being utterly depleted of strength. It's a chore to answer the phone. You can't bear to hear the doorbell. You can't make it to the mailbox and back.

Much to my surprise, my friend Bill responded to Alton's misfortune by leading him in a powerful, insightful prayer right there at the table. And before we left the restaurant, Bill had volunteered to meet with Alton on a weekly basis for ongoing mutual encouragement and prayer. I'm sure you can guess the outcome of the meetings these two men had. With the passing of time, both men emerged from their depression, began to see new possibilities for reviving their careers, and ultimately became employed again.

God's method of helping Bill break out of his depression was found in ministering to Alton. Had Bill remained isolated and stuck in his own world of problems, his recovery might have dragged on indefinitely. It's easy for that to happen when you're hurting. You can't see past your problems. You don't have the time or energy or mental space to care for anyone else. Yet, Bill looked past that. He became involved in caring for someone else, and when he did so, his own clouds of depression began to lift.

THE KEY TO BEATING YOUR DEPRESSION

What about you? How are you handling your difficulties? Would others say that you spend the majority of time getting from others or giving to others? The key that God will use to unlock your depression and discouragement may very well be getting involved in helping someone else. Consider the following biblical principles of helping others.

1. God is glorified when we help others in need. After you experienced salvation in Jesus Christ, God left you here on earth for a reason. Part of that purpose is to express His love to others who need what you have found in Jesus Christ. Study what Jesus said in Matthew 25:34–40.

> Then the King will say to those on His right, "Come, you who are blessed of My Father, inherit the kingdom prepared for you from the foundation of the world. For I was hungry, and you gave Me something to eat; I was thirsty and you gave Me something to drink; I was a stranger, and you invited Me in; naked, and you clothed Me; I was sick, and you visited Me; I was in prison, and you came to Me." Then the righteous will answer Him, "Lord, when did we see You hungry, and feed You, or thirsty, and give you something to drink? And when did we see You a stranger, and invite You in, or naked, and clothe You? When did we see You sick, or in prison, and come to You?" The King will answer and say to them, "Truly I say to you, to the extent that you did it to one of these brothers of Mine, even to the least of them, you did it to Me."

Few things create a more effective witness for Christ than reaching out to help others *when you yourself are hurting and in need.* The world cannot understand or explain that behavior because serving others is a divine act of humility. We cannot serve others in the strength of our flesh; rather, we become empowered by the Holy Spirit who dwells within us.

Notice in the passage above that the righteous didn't even know it was the Lord whom they were serving. They weren't serving to earn "kudos" with God. Rather, they were serving out of genuine care and compassion. God gets the honor and glory when you serve in His power and Spirit, and seldom is that more clearly seen than in your own time of need (see 2 Corinthians 12:9).

2. *God uses our suffering to prepare us to serve others.*

Bill was able to relate to Alton because he had been down that same path before. Indeed, Bill was still struggling with depression and career issues. But notice that God didn't wait to work through Bill's life until everything was patched up and perfectly back in order. If that were the case, God would never accomplish anything through people, precisely because we're all in the process of being repaired and refurbished in our lives. Instead, God used the suffering in Bill's life as an entrance into Alton's life and as the common bond of encouragement between the two.

No doubt God has prepared someone among your acquaintances to receive the encouragement and insights you have to offer, and you are qualified to speak to the person simply because of all you have gone through. Look at what Paul said to the Corinthians: "Blessed be the God and Father of our Lord Jesus Christ, the Father of mercies and God of all comfort; who comforts us in all our affliction so that we will be able to comfort those who are in any affliction with the comfort with which we ourselves are comforted by God" (2 Corinthians 1:3–4).

God's plan is for you to experience His love, comfort, and hope and for you to share those same experiences with others in need. His greatest desire is for you to be closer to Him and draw others closer to Him through your life experiences.

THE BENEFITS OF HELPING OTHERS

Two things happen when you reach out to others and become involved in their lives. The first effect is obvious: The other person is encouraged and built up because you took the time to care. Your thoughtful word or gesture may snatch a depressed person back from the brink of suicide. Don't underestimate what you can mean to another hurting person.

The second effect may not be as evident, however, because it's a paradox. *The more you give away, the more you will receive.* You will benefit from the encounter. Your load will get lighter as you dare to reach out to someone who desperately needs your love, attention, and care, and you will experience the following benefits.

1. Helping others confirms that you are living under the lordship of Jesus Christ. There is no logical explanation for giving, encouraging, and sharing with needy people when your own life is under tremendous strain. The way of the world is to be preoccupied with number one first (you); the way of Christ is to serve others first. Listen to the way Paul stated this principle: "Do nothing from selfishness or empty conceit, but with humility of mind regard one another as more important than yourselves; do not merely look out for your own personal interests, but also for the interests of others" (Philippians 2:3–4).

Notice that Paul did not say to apply this principle to your life only after all your needs are met, or when your "cup is full" or you have nothing else to do with your time and money. Instead, he states this as a lifestyle principle that applies under all circumstances.

The witness of helping others will be particularly comforting to your family because they will see you are receiving your instructions from God. And the world will be at a loss to explain what you're doing. People will literally come up to you and ask, "How could you do that? How could you forgive?"

Suddenly you will have an effective, powerful witness for Jesus Christ. You will be able to tell others about Jesus Christ and how He is meeting your needs, how faithful He is, and what a "good shepherd" He is—all from personal experience. And the outcome of your life will be much better than if you had remained in control.

I remember when I first turned my life over to Jesus Christ. I literally told people, "Look, I'm just God's mouthpiece. God is in control of my life and I'm going to do what He tells me to do." To be honest, I was a little embarrassed at times because I was a new Christian. People remembered me "the old way" and thought I had gone crazy. When you commit to helping others, you confirm that you are living under the lordship of Jesus Christ. People will know who is in control of your life.

2. *Helping others relieves stress.* Stress is a major factor to cope with when you have financial difficulties. I know. Through the years I have owned many companies, and I know what it's like to be down, discouraged, and depressed. I remember a construction company I owned in the early seventies that took a nose-dive following a downturn in the economy. For more than two years I fought to keep that business alive, but I just couldn't make it work. When I hit bottom, I owed more than a million dollars and had a debt service of $10,000 a month. So I'm no stranger to stress. But I also know that helping others can relieve stress.

When I get stressed out, my natural response is to sit down and eat, two activities that are exactly the opposite of what I should be doing. I should be exercising and minimizing my food intake. And instead of sitting around whining and moping, I should be finding someone to help. Dr. Frank Minirth and Dr. Paul Meier have written a great book called *Happiness Is a Choice*, in which they identify finding someone else to help as one of the seven cures for depression.

Stress can turn people away from you, make it hard to concentrate, and even interfere with your ability to worship God. Are you unable to listen to what your pastor is preaching each Sunday? Have you noticed people "backing off" in their relationship with you, people like your wife, children, friends, church members, or co-workers (if you have a job)? Unresolved stress can drive the very people away that you need to become more deeply involved with. After all, how often do you enter a room full of people and look for the most stressed-out person to hang out with?

3. *Clear thinking often results from helping others.* How, you ask? Stress, depression, and pressure can distort your thinking. Molehills become formidable, towering mountains. I heard someone say once that 95 percent of the problems we worry about never happen. We brace ourselves for the worst, and it never comes. We're armed for battle, ready to confront, but nothing happens. We tell ourselves:

- God is intentionally causing this chaos in our lives.
- We are utter failures and good for nothing.
- We need something that we can't live without.
- No one loves us; in fact, we're unlovable.
- Things will never change or get any better.

Left unchecked, negative thoughts bounce around in our brains like balls in a pinball machine. Without healthy interaction with other people, twisted thinking prompts us to unwise actions.

Instead, with Christ at the controls of your life, you will become an instrument of His love and power. You will begin to see the pain and hurt others are experiencing, and your predicament will shrink as you discover that others are struggling also, and that you have something to offer them. And, much to your delight, you might discover that others have something to offer you. King Solomon put it like this in the book of Proverbs: "Iron sharpens iron, so one man sharpens another" (Proverbs 27:17).

As you help others, balance and perspective are restored to your thoughts, especially your perceptions of your problems. Just when you think your problems are the worst, let God introduce you to someone who has it worse. Visit a children's hospital. Listen to the elderly in a nursing home. You're not the only one with problems, and many have situations much worse than yours.

4. *Helping others illustrates the biblical principle of stewardship.* It's easy in America to slip into the mentality of what our "rights" are. We begin thinking we have a right to a job, a right to a nice house and car, or a right to good health (and health care coverage). Once in a mentality of "ownership," we think God is punishing us if we don't get what we want, *when* we want it. We might even think He doesn't hear us or care about our needs.

In contrast is the mentality of a steward. A steward recognizes that God owns everything and that he is simply left in charge of what God has entrusted to him. Because He is sovereign and never makes mistakes, God is free to do as He pleases with material goods. He entrusts much to some people and just a little to others.

He can give and He can take away. And because God is holy and righteous, He always does the right thing.

When we're committed to helping others, we're free from envy or jealousy over what material things other people have. Nor do we have to regret losing what we used to have. Someone asked John D. Rocke-feller's accountant how much Rockefeller left after he died, and the accountant replied, *"All of it."* That's exactly what you're going to do. There will come a point in time when you have to leave it all. It doesn't make much sense to cling to material possessions, to assume you'll be here forever, or to build your values around material gain. The Bible says it all belongs to God, not you.

By helping others, you'll discover a new sense of gratitude about what you *do* have, and less remorse about what you *don't* have.

HOW TO START HELPING OTHERS

It's time to move beyond the theoretical. It's time for you to reach out to someone else, find out what his or her needs are, and find a way to help that person, for his or her benefit and for yours. I know that you're hurting, but you're not alone. There are thousands and thousands of hurting people around you. It could be your next-door neighbor, the checker at the supermar-ket, the man who runs the gas station, or the young person who sits in front of you at church. Hurting peo-ple are all around you.

I know what it's like to be scared to death, depressed, and seeing no way out. The last thing you want to do is go out and find someone to help; your own problems are too big. They seem bigger than anyone else's. I know there are a dozen reasons why you can't get involved. That's what Satan wants you to think. He wants to keep you isolated and immobilized . . . stuck right where you are. Those thoughts are not true, however.

If you don't help people in need, who will? There are no "knights in shining armor" to come to their rescue. All of us have needs. God's plan is for needy people to help needy people while relying on His strength and using His resources, and that leads to the first step you must take in helping others.

STEP #1 — ASK GOD FOR COURAGE AND SOMEONE TO HELP

If you're not used to helping others, you're going to need courage to be open yourself as well as to hear the incredible hurts other people are experiencing. Courage is simply the ability to face danger or fears with bravery and confidence. With God in control of your life, He will give you both of those qualities and more.

If you can't think of anyone in need, ask God to show you one person. Just start with one. Now that doesn't mean you can sit down in your favorite chair, watch TV, and wait for God to plop someone on your doorstep. Instead, after you have prayed, circulate with people, and listen to what they are saying. Go to where hurting people typically gather. Ask God to give you a ministry to someone at church, your favorite restaurant, or at the mall. Go to your pastor, ask him for direction, and tell him why you're motivated to help others.

STEP #2 — LISTEN CAREFULLY

When you find that particular person, move past

small talk by asking questions like, "What is going on in your life?", "How is business?", "How are things going?", or "How can I be praying for you?" You might tell your personal story to get things started and speak frankly about some of the problems you have faced, as well as how God has helped you.

Listen with both your mind and your heart because sometimes the person will say one thing, but his or her heart will truly be saying something else. A great way to practice this is by listening to your spouse.

Beyond your personal story, however, I don't recommend giving advice. Your job is simply to listen, not to "fix." Besides, your friend may be hurting so much he or she can't hear advice. Instead, he or she may just need to have someone listen and care about the intensity of pain. As the person shares, I also recommend that you inwardly begin praying, asking the Holy Spirit for discernment and guidance. God will supply the right word of encouragement for your friend. This makes your listening two-dimensional, since you're listening to your friend and to the Holy Spirit simultaneously. It's work, and you have to practice to sharpen your skills, but you can do it.

HOW REACHING OUT
TRANSFORMED WALTER'S GRIEF

Walter's world caved in on him in a matter of months. Because his wife of forty-three years had terminal cancer, he lost his business. He simply could not run the store, keep the books, maintain inventory, and spend time with his wife. Since there was no one else to take care of her and since she was his top priority, Walter chose the latter. The business just folded.

In a matter of months, she was completely overrun with the cancer and died, leaving Walter without his lifelong mate and best friend. The two had done everything together, and he missed her terribly in his daily routine. He grieved for months.

One day, Walter read in the newspaper that a man about his age had lost his wife in an automobile accident. He didn't know the man, but, nonetheless, Walter hurt for him because he knew the shock and pain all too well. As Walter quietly breathed a prayer for the surviving husband, the Holy Spirit dropped an idea on his heart: *Why not visit the man? Perhaps I could encourage him after the shock wears off,* Walter thought.

He waited for several weeks to pass, and then, without calling, Walter drove up to the man's house. After he introduced himself and disclosed the reason for his visit, Walter was invited to come in and chat for a while. The chat became a visit, and before they knew it, the two men had talked through the entire afternoon, into the evening, and all the way up to midnight. Each shared memories of his wife, the loneliness he was gripped with, and how he was going to get back on his feet again. Before Walter left, the two had become good friends.

They began fishing together, going out to favorite restaurants for supper, and sharing each other's load. "Bear one another's burdens, and thereby fulfill the law of Christ" (Galatians 6:2). Walter reached out to someone in need and was blessed in return.

GOD'S PLAN IS FOR YOU TO HELP OTHERS

I am challenging you to make a commitment to help someone else. Don't wait until all your problems disappear, because that will never happen. Someone in your world needs your encouragement today. If you can't think of anyone in need, ask God, ask your pastor, or ask at church. You won't have to wait long to find someone. Your inability to think of anyone else in need may be indicative of just how self-centered your life has become, and how out of touch you are with the rest of the world around you.

By the way, I'm not asking you to abandon your responsibilities at home or neglect your work (if you're working). Just try to make time each day, if only a little bit, to find someone to encourage. It could be as simple as visiting the widow in your neighborhood and cutting her grass.

Helping someone else will get your mind off yourself and be an important step to getting out of the bottom of the barrel. Sign your commitment below, date it, and get started.

I have made a commitment to go out and help someone else so that Jesus Christ might be glorified in my life, knowing that He will be pleased by my actions.

_____   _____

YOUR SIGNATURE   DATE

CONCLUDING PRINCIPLE:

*Helping others is
part of your solution.*

CHAPTER 18

I'VE DONE
ALL THAT

But I've tried all that and it doesn't work, Van. Just look.
I'm still stuck at the bottom of the barrel, and I'm still
not experiencing peace and joy in my life. As you've
been reading this book, is that what you've been telling
yourself? Have you been clicking through these chapters, discounting them one at a time by saying, "Yeah,
but Van doesn't know my situation. These ideas won't
work for me. Who could have peace and joy in the
middle of this mess?"

If you're thinking that you can only have peace and
joy when all your problems disappear, let me tell you
something. *You'll never have peace and joy in your life.*
That's because you'll never be problem-free in this life.
Neither will I or anybody else you meet. "For man is
born for trouble, as sparks fly upward" (Job 5:7).

The good news is, you can be filled to overflowing
with peace and joy regardless of how terrible your
problems are. My prayer for you is not only that God
will deliver you from the bottom of the barrel in life;
but also that you will experience God's peace and joy *in
the process of getting out of the hole.* Few things are as
beautiful or compelling in life as a man or woman who

can overcome personal tragedies and setbacks and praise God anyway. That's a powerful witness for Christ. When I think back over my life, I believe I have been most profoundly impacted by people who were filled with peace and joy in the midst of incredibly dismal circumstances. The reason? Because it was so clear that God was with them, flooding their souls with His strength and power! I can get excited about God giving me His strength, power, peace, and joy. Can you?

Wouldn't you enjoy being like that? Wouldn't you like to have people look up to you, respect you, and praise God because of your ability to demonstrate peace and joy in the middle of adversity? Let me tell you something. You can't do it on your own. Like a child, you'll have to be humble and receive these holy gifts of peace and joy from God. The good news is that you don't have to wait. You can have them today.

PEACE AND JOY ARE GIFTS FROM GOD

Even though it may take years, maybe even a lifetime, for you to recover from your predicament, peace and joy can be yours right now. God's desire is to give those two precious qualities to you, and like your salvation, all you have to do is receive them: "But the fruit of the Spirit is love, joy, peace, patience, kindness, goodness, faithfulness, gentleness, self-control" (Galatians 5:22–23a).

When the Holy Spirit dwells within you, His fruits will begin to manifest themselves in your life. Like a seed planted in the spring, these fruits, or evidences of His presence, will be planted within your heart although they may not be evident to others immediately. But you'll know because you'll be experiencing them daily. The intimacy of His holy presence in all of your thoughts and actions will satisfy you deep down to the core of your soul.

Your circumstances may not change very much. They may not change at all, or they could get even worse. But God can still change you and flood your heart with peace and joy. In fact, His desire is to do that very work in you *right now*. Why not just bow your head and ask God to flood your life with peace and joy?

Maintaining His peace and joy will probably be a challenge for you. It's that way for me too. Rather than a one-time event, I need God to fill me with peace and joy day by day, sometimes minute by minute. That's because there are many factors working to destroy peace of mind and joy of heart. As you read over the items listed below, you may discover why you have not been experiencing peace and joy up to this point in your life.

OBSTACLES TO PEACE AND JOY

1. *A negative attitude will stifle your peace and joy.* Sometimes people get "burned" in life and conclude that things will never be right again. No matter how many blessings and victories God sends their way, they see everything from a negative, defeatist point of view. Such an attitude will stifle your ability to have peace and joy in your life. Like oil and water, they don't mix. Either peace and joy will dissolve a negative attitude, or vice versa.

I counseled a businessman once who was facing financial disaster. After listening to him for four or five hours, it was evident to me that this man was not going to get out from under his financial collapse until he changed his negative attitude. Every idea that I raised or suggestion I made got shot down. I felt like I was in a skeet shooting tournament. *Boom! Boom! Boom!* "That won't work. Forget it. I've tried that idea, too. No way—that would never work here." One by one, he blasted every effort I made to help.

A habit of negative thinking may reflect a lack of faith in God or some deep, emotional wound from your past. Get your focus off what can't happen, and begin to consider all the wonderful things God can do for you. If you've accepted Jesus Christ as your Lord and Savior, He's your new leader. And He can make anything happen. Think about what Matthew 28:18 means. "All authority has been given to Me in heaven and on earth."

With Christ at the helm in your life, *anything* can happen. Since He can righteously do whatever He wants, just go ahead and chuck that negative-thinking trash out the window. It belongs in the garbage can because it is stealing the peace and joy that God intends for you from your life.

2. *Confusing God's preparation with punishment will take away your peace and joy.* I don't know what I'm going to be facing tomorrow, next week, or next year, but God does. And in His grace and wisdom, He's taking me through some things and allowing me to suffer much longer than I desire in order to prepare me for the future. Like a good football coach, God knows that practicing full-throttle will get me prepared for game day and "the test."

However, if you mistakenly interpret His plan to prepare you as punishment, two things are likely to happen. (1) Rather than being grateful and trusting that God is at work in your life, it will be easy to grow bitter and angry with God. Instead of drawing near to Him in faith, you'll find yourself pulling away from Him. (2) Because you rebel against His preparation in your life, neither will you be prepared for the future. It's sort of like school—if you don't do your homework and study for the test, you won't be ready for the exam. If the football team never practices, it will never be ready for game day.

Scripture promises, "Much more then, having now been justified by His blood, we shall be saved from the wrath of God through Him" (Romans 5:9). So if you're facing difficulties, don't think that God is trying to punish you. He's poured out His wrath on His Son Jesus at the cross. Instead, the truth is that He's trying to pour out His peace and joy in your life.

That doesn't mean that He won't allow difficulties to come your way, because He will. And that doesn't mean He will never discipline you to get you back on track. But as a believer, nothing in life can touch you except by the permission of God. And when hard times come, trust that God is still in control and that He will bring you through. Here's the way the writer of Hebrews put it: "All discipline for the moment seems not to be joyful, but sorrowful; yet to those who have been trained by it, afterwards it yields the peaceful fruit of righteousness" (Hebrews 12:11).

If you misunderstand God's discipline and preparation in your life as His punishment, His peace and joy will fade from your heart. In fact, you may never fully understand why you're facing the circumstances you see. I'm sure that Joseph, David, Moses, and Paul faced things they didn't understand. But that's the nature of faith. Faith beckons you to trust God where you cannot see and understand.

3. *Reaping what you have sown may make it harder to experience peace and joy.* You know that you don't reap in the same season you sow, don't you? Think about a farmer who sows in the spring, but reaps in the summer. You may be reaping what you have sown for years, and if so, that will make it harder to experience peace and joy. But you can, nonetheless.

You may say to yourself, "OK. I've stopped doing what I was doing. I've stopped cheating people, or I've stopped lying to people. I've started being honest with my banker and my employees, and I'm going to start doing it God's way. I'm going to love my wife."

And with your new resolve, you expect nothing but smooth sailing. Perhaps you expect your wife to suddenly think you've hung the moon or for your kids to sit up and behave or quit talking back.

It seldom happens that way. You can't control other people. Even after you get right with God, you can only influence them, but you can't make them do everything you want. Instead, you will likely reap what you have been sowing, and that harvest may come in for a while. How long the harvest lasts is not your choice. The only thing you can control at this point is what kind of seeds you will sow now and how many of them will be sown in the future.

> Do not be deceived, God is not mocked; for whatever a man sows, this he will also reap. For the one who sows to his own flesh shall from the flesh reap corruption, but the one who sows to the Spirit shall from the Spirit reap eternal life. (Galatians 6:7–8)

For they sow the wind and they reap the whirlwind.
(Hosea 8:7a)

You may continue to reap what you have sown for
a time. Don't let that fact, however, steal your peace
and joy away. God will have a witness through you
even in the middle of an ugly harvest.

4. *You can resist the peace and joy God offers.* Some
people want to be pampered like children. Others
childishly resist taking responsibility for their lives by
making unwise choices. The bottom line is that you
can choose to accept or reject God's provision of peace
and joy. Once you're in Christ, you have a choice in the
matter.

I've worked with people who are just plain miserable. I'm convinced that's how they like to be. It's
ingrained in them. I know because I've been that way
myself; I remember times when I had my mind made
up to be miserable.

It reminds me of a little five-year-old boy who pout-
ed all the way through his birthday party. He didn't get
his way about something and he decided he was going
to be miserable. When the rest of the kids sang "Happy
Birthday," he frowned and acted like a brat. Everyone at
the party—the little boy's parents, grandparents, neighbors, and friends—wished that he would enjoy the
occasion. But instead, he chose to pout.

Are you *choosing* not to experience all that God has
for you, maybe to punish yourself? Listen carefully to
the way the apostle Paul prayed for the church at Eph-
esus: "I pray that the eyes of your heart may be enlight-
ened, so that you will know what is the hope of His
calling, what are the riches of the glory of His inheri-

tance in the saints, and what is the surpassing greatness of His power toward us who believe" (Ephesians 1:18–19a).

God has so much in store for you. Open your heart to receive the fullness of joy and peace that He desires to flood into you.

5. *Unwillingness to accept the role God has given you will undermine your peace and joy.* Maybe you don't like who you are or what you look like. I doubt you like what God is doing in your circumstances. Most of us would choose the easiest way out of things, after all. Perhaps you're trapped in a bad partnership or marriage. You didn't have a choice about who your parents were or you didn't get accepted to the college you hoped for or maybe someone really close to you died. There are a lot of factors in life that you don't have any control over. Your unwillingness to accept those factors, which God has allowed for whatever reason, will eat away at your peace of mind and joy in heart.

Think about this. If you're unwilling to accept the role that God has given you in life, it's like telling Him He doesn't know what He's doing or that He's the source of bad, evil things. Actually, the opposite is true. God is in the business of making good things out of bad things (Romans 8:28).

There are some conditions in Romans 8:28, namely, that you have to love God and submit yourself to His purpose. What you see as a bad situation, God sees as an opportunity for demonstrating His power, glory, and honor. His specialty is overcoming evil with good.

Let me tell you what I'm impressed by. I don't admire people and say, "Look what they've done while they're on top." I admire people who start with nothing, are certainly not in a power position, and are not able to speak well, but who trust God to make something of their lives. And you know what? He uses them in ways I can't believe. I get convicted when I see someone who has nothing and has been beaten down give everything.

Don't be resentful of the role God has given you in life. Accept His plan. Submit to His will. Resisting God's provision for you will not only grieve Him, but it will undermine your ability to experience peace and joy in your life.

If you're not experiencing peace and joy, is it due to any of the reasons above? Are you fighting against God's provision instead of accepting it? I've known people who have lost children to death right after birth; others, while they were in grammar school; yet others, when their children were in high school, or when they were married. I've known people who have lost grandchildren in terrible tragedies. I've known people who've lost fortunes, power, prestige, you name it, and they just keep on being submissive and thankful to God. Most of all, they don't waver in their joyful heart and peace of mind.

What about you? Are you frustrated because you're at the bottom of the barrel?

I'm not sure a Christian has a "bottom" or lowest point in life, because God's hand can always reach lower to save you. No matter how low you go, God can still bring about His best for you. He can begin His best work in you, bringing peace and joy, precisely at the moment when you decide to let Him in.

Here's what I want you to do. I know that at this point you may be weary of do-gooders, of shortcuts, of easy answers, and lists of one-two-three things to do. I want you to pray through the things you've read in this book so far. Ask God for help to understand them. And then ask God for peace and joy in your life. They don't come from money in the bank. Peace and joy come from God.

I challenge you to accept by faith today the gift of peace and joy that God desires to flood your soul with. Will you do that? Will you sign the line below and date it?

I am truly hungry for God's peace in my mind and His joy in my heart, and I hereby ask for them by faith.

_____   _____

Your signature   Date

CONCLUDING PRINCIPLE:

> *Peace and joy are*
> *in the heart, not*
> *in the pocketbook.*

CHAPTER 19

HOW TO ACCOMPLISH THE IMPOSSIBLE

You're mistaken and you're setting yourself up for failure if you think you can accomplish everything set forth in this book on your own. You cannot. You cannot rebuild your own life. You cannot make yourself feel peace and joy. You cannot make your wife love you again. On every side, you're surrounded by limitations.

So what's the point of the book? you ask. *Why grapple with all these principles if they're impossible to execute?* There is a way. In fact, as best as I can tell, there is only one way. Here's the secret.

You can't do these things on your own. Only God can accomplish the impossible in your life. The only thing you can do is resolve to make yourself available to God by submitting to His sovereign will.

There. That's the secret you must know to get back on your feet again. You must let the Lord Jesus Christ bring His resurrection power to bear on your life circumstances and let Him live through you. Here's how the apostle Paul said it in the book of Galatians: "I have been crucified with Christ; and it is no longer I who live, but Christ lives in me; and the life which I now live in the flesh I live by faith in the Son of God, who loved me, and gave Himself up for me" (Galatians 2:20).

The great missionary to China, J. Hudson Taylor, called it the "exchanged life." By that, he meant that each person is called to give up his or her life, or exchange it, for the life of Jesus Christ in us. In his book *They Found the Secret* (Zondervan), V. Raymond Edman summarizes the exchanged life this way:

> What is the exchanged life? Really, it is not some thing: it is some One. It is the indwelling of the Lord Jesus Christ made real and rewarding by the Holy Spirit. There is no more glorious reality in all the world. It is life with a capital L. It is new life for old. It is rejoicing for weariness, and radiance for dreariness. It is strength for weakness, and steadiness for uncertainty. It is triumph even through tears, and tenderness of heart instead of touchiness. It is lowliness of spirit instead of self-exaltation, and loveliness of life because of the presence of the altogether Lovely One.[1]

If you have been overwhelmed, even after reading this book, feeling like there is a crushing weight on your shoulders, pushing you down, down, down to the bottom of the barrel, you need to hear this. Jesus Christ has the power to raise you up. Better yet, *He wants to*. He desires to and He will give you the strength. That's because you are the heart-throb of His being. He loves you so much He freely gave Himself for you on the cross. And now He wants to lift you up!

When you choose to let Him take control of your life, you'll begin to experience the exchanged life. And here's even more good news. *When you trust God for the outcome of your life, you'll see God-sized results!*

LOOK WHAT HAPPENED WHEN TYLER BRADLEY TRUSTED GOD

Tyler Bradley was a model Christian businessman who, for years, ran his small manufacturing business on an island south of Florida. Because he followed biblical principles in his work, he and the business were blessed by God. His employees loved and respected him dearly, and Tyler even discipled several after business hours. His suppliers admired him. Tyler was debt-free both in his business and in his family. He, his wife, and their three children were a model family in their church and community.

Then Hurricane Andrew struck, and Tyler lost everything except his family. His manufacturing plant, his income, his home, and his cars were all totally destroyed. Yet he began to praise the Lord.

Two thoughts triggered his praise.

Tyler praised God that his wife and children were spared. Some in his neighborhood had lost loved ones, and while Tyler was saddened for them, he praised God that his family survived.

But Tyler also praised God for the freedom that came from simply being a steward of material things, not an owner. You see, if Tyler had believed everything he had—his house, nice furnishings, his cars, his business—was all his to own, and thus his to get back, perhaps he would have panicked. After all, it took all of his career to get him where he was.

But as a steward, Tyler realized that God had provided all these things for his enjoyment and witness here on earth. Like the biblical character Job, Tyler believed that if God, in His righteousness, gave these things, God could also righteously take them away. Job put it his way: "Naked I came from my mother's womb, and naked I shall return there. The Lord gave and the Lord has taken away. Blessed be the name of the Lord" (Job 1:21). Also: "'Shall we indeed accept good from God and not accept adversity?' In all this Job did not sin with his lips" (Job 2:10b).

There's more to Tyler's story. Weeks passed, and Tyler busied himself with helping his family, his neighbors, and his employees get their lives back together again. With no opportunity of rebuilding his own manufacturing plant, Tyler instead took a job as a carpenter and worked to repair some buildings owned by William.

One day, while Tyler was clearing debris, he and William struck up a conversation, and William learned more about Tyler's background. William particularly noticed the strength of Tyler's faith, his peace of mind (even though his plant had been destroyed), and Tyler's obvious management capabilities.

Two weeks later, an attorney representing William appeared with an incredible offer at the apartment that Tyler and his family were renting. The attorney informed Tyler that William intended to rebuild Tyler's plant, equip it, and lease it to him for *$1.00 a year* for the next ten years. After that, William would allow him to purchase the plant at its depreciated value over the next ten-year period with no interest.

Needless to say, Tyler and his family fell on their knees and praised God for this turn of events. Now that's a God-sized answer to prayer! Only God could work a deal like this—there simply is no other explanation.

WHO'S IN CHARGE, ANYWAY?

If you continue to live your life by your will, you'll be limited by your meager power and energy. If you live the exchanged life, where you present your body to Christ as a living sacrifice (Romans 12:1–2), you'll live with God's limitless power and abundance inside of you. And since there's no way your heart, your mind, and your body can contain all of God's power, you know what happens? *It spills out of you so that everyone around you is touched by the power of God!* You can't stop it—it just happens!

Now you may say, "Van, I've tried that business of selling out to God before, and look where I am. It doesn't work."

I've thought that too, and so have others I've worked with. But when I look back, I can see that I really hadn't turned everything over to God. Instead, I had gotten to a point where I was so frustrated and angry that I'd say to God, "OK, You take it. I'm sick of it." In reality, I was only attempting to manipulate God, trying to get Him to give me a hint of what He wanted to do, but let me take it from there and fill in all the details.

That won't work. God wants all of you. If you want to see God accomplish great things in your life, there's only one way to let it happen. You have to live by God's power in your life. You have to relinquish your will and let God have His will in your life.

One of the best resources I've seen to help train a person in growing in an exchanged life relationship with God is a workbook called *Experiencing God* by Henry T. Blackaby and Claude V. King (Life Way Press). It's basically a discipleship training manual that will help you to live out the principles I've shared in this book. Since it's being used for small group studies in churches across America, you might pull together a group of people in your own church and find God's blessing that way.

With God in control of your life, you'll have everything you need to serve Him. In a little booklet called *How to Live on Christ,* Harriet Beecher Stowe clarifies this very point, basing her point on John 15:1–5.

> How does the branch bear fruit? Not by incessant effort for sunshine and air; not by vain struggles for those vivifying influences which give beauty to the blossom, and verdure to the leaf: it simply abides in the vine, in silent and undisturbed union, and blossoms and fruit appear as of spontaneous growth.
>
> How, then, shall a Christian bear fruit? By efforts and struggles to obtain that which is freely given; by meditations on watchfulness, on prayer, on action, on temptation, and on dangers? No: there must be a full concentration of the thoughts and affections of Christ; a complete surrender of the whole being to Him; a constant looking to Him for grace. Christians in whom these dispositions are once firmly fixed go on calmly as the infant borne in the arms of its mother. Christ reminds them of every duty in its time and place, reproves them for every error, counsels them in every difficulty, excites them to every needful activity. . . . Their hope and trust rest solely on what He is willing and able to do for them; on nothing that they suppose themselves able and willing to do for Him.[2]

DO IT IN GOD'S STRENGTH

When you live an exchanged life with God, when

He says, "Turn to the left," you understand what He wants and you turn to the left. You don't ask why, when, where, or anything else. You just do it because He said to, and you trust Him for the outcome.

When you live the exchanged life, you're not using God, trying to manipulate Him, or second-guessing Him. Whatever He provides you in the way of income is enough—you don't have to beg and whine for more. That's why this book is not about how to get more money out of God; rather, it's about how to get more of God into your life. And when that happens, you have enough! You'll know what it means to be satisfied and content.

THE COMMITMENT

Are you willing to lay everything on the line with God? Can you trust Him for the outcomes of all the problems you're facing today? You can't do it on your own. You can do it with God in the driver's seat of your life. Are you willing to say, "Not me, Lord, but You"? Can you pray the following prayer with integrity?

"Lord, do whatever You want with me to make me Yours. I want to be totally controlled by You, and I want You to do whatever You have to in my life so that I have a totally yielded life."

I prayed that God would have it all. Amen.

_____   _____
Your signature   Date

CONCLUDING PRINCIPLE:

*If Jesus Christ
lives in you, let
Him have His way.*

1. V. Raymond Edman, *They Found the Secret: Twenty Transformed Lives That Reveal a Touch of Eternity* (Grand Rapids: Zondervan, 1984), xiii–xiv.

2. Ibid., 6.

CHAPTER 20
THE BADGE OF VICTORY

When you run a race and win, the reward is yours. If you're committed to applying the principles in this book, you'll be a winner. God wants you to live a victorious life and experience His peace and joy in spite of your problems. That's because He can make you a powerful witness to the world right in the middle of your turmoil. The key to experiencing that victory is your faith and obedience to what God has said in His Word. Consider the following passages.

But He said, "On the contrary, blessed are those who hear the word of God and observe it." (Luke 11:28)

Jesus answered and said, "If anyone loves Me, he will keep My word; and My Father will love him, and We will come to him, and make Our abode with him." (John 14:23)

If you keep My commandments, you will abide in My love; just as I have kept My Father's commandments, and abide in His love. (John 15:10)

But thanks be to God, who gives us the victory through our Lord Jesus Christ. (1 Corinthians 15:57)

GET THIS STRAIGHT!

I don't do all the things that I've talked about in this book all the time. There are times when I become angry, have my own pity party, don't forgive others the way I should, or blame somebody else. I'm sure there are times when I don't do exactly what Jesus would do, and I know I don't reach out and help as many people as I should.

But I am better than I used to be, and as a result, I'm not complicating my life the way I used to. I'm part of the solution more often and less often a contributor to problems.

You won't be able to do everything mentioned in this book, either. You'll struggle, just as I continue to struggle in some areas. That's OK. Just don't give up. Do what you can today, and then start over in the morning. You're not going to be sinless and perfect all the time. Just don't give up when you blow it. Stick with it and you will experience God's rewards, not only in the life to come, but day by day.

LOOK AT SOME OF THE REWARDS

If you're willing to trust God and obey Him in all that He says to do, just look at all the benefits He promises to you.

1. *Peace and joy.* You may have financial troubles, but you can have the peace and joy of the Lord anyway. Those are gifts that another human being cannot take from you. You can give them up, but another person cannot take them.

2. *Hope.* When you obey God's Word, He will revive your hope. That's because you have a deeply rooted confidence that He is at work in your life. Just listen to what the apostle Paul said to the Ephesians: "Now to Him who is able to do exceeding abundantly beyond all that we ask or think, according to the power that works within us, to Him be the glory in the church and in Christ Jesus to all generations forever and ever. Amen" (Ephesians 3:20–21).

If God is able to do "exceeding abundantly" beyond what you ask or think, maybe you need to grow bolder when you ask Him for something, or even consider what He is able to do. That kind of thinking —believing that God is truly in charge of all things, and that He can do anything He wants—inspires hope.

3. *You'll have a constant companion.* Other people will probably forsake you or turn their backs on you when times get tough. Not the Lord. He says in Joshua 1:5, "I will be with you; I will not fail you or forsake you." When you have failed, He will be there to help you pick up the pieces. Because His love for you is unconditional, you cannot earn it. And if you can't earn it, neither can you do something to make Him stop loving you.

4. *You won't have to be frightened anymore.* When you belong to God, He is your Shepherd, and the "good shepherd" protects His sheep. You don't have to fear the IRS, your creditors, the bank, or whatever tomorrow might bring. Your life is in the hands of the Lord. He's already in tomorrow, next week, and next year. If you've committed all your worldly goods, yes, even your life and family, under the lordship of Jesus Christ, what can be done to you? Paul put it like this in Romans 8:

What then shall we say to these things? If God is for us,
who is against us? He who did not spare His own Son,
but delivered Him over for us all, how will He not also
with Him freely give us all things? . . . Who will separate
us from the love of Christ? Will tribulation, or distress,
or persecution, or famine, or nakedness, or peril, or
sword? . . . But in all these things we overwhelmingly
conquer through Him who loved us. (Romans 8:31–32,
35, 37)

5. *You won't feel like a failure.* There's no need to
continue blaming others, because God doesn't make
failures. When you trust God, *you cannot fail.* Satan will
work overtime to convince you that you'll never
amount to anything, but God is working just as hard to
get you on your feet again. Here's what He says through
the prophet Jeremiah.

> "For I know the plans that I have for you," declares the
> Lord, "plans for welfare and not for calamity to give you
> a future and a hope. Then you will call upon Me and
> come and pray to Me, and I will listen to you. You will
> seek Me and find Me when you search for Me with all
> your heart. I will be found by you," declares the Lord.
> (Jeremiah 29:11–14)

6. *Many other benefits come from obeying God's principles.* Just think of all that God can bless you with if
you obey what He says.

You'll have a long-range plan for your life, not
some "quick fix" solution that will have you back in
trouble again this time next year.

You'll be equipped to help other hurting, lonely
people with their problems.

You'll be able to deal honestly with creditors.

You'll experience contentment, because you've learned to wait on the Lord.

You'll be forgiven of your sins.

You'll know where you're going to spend eternity (see John 14:3).

You'll have new meaning and purpose for your remaining days here on earth.

The rewards that God holds in store for those who love Him simply defy description.

Here's the way Paul said it in 1 Corinthians: "Just as it is written, 'Things which eye has not seen and ear has not heard, and which have not entered the heart of man, all that God has prepared for those who love Him'" (1 Corinthians 2:9).

I praise God that you have a desire to follow Him and live a life with the peace and joy that He has for you. "Keep on keeping on" serving Him: *your victory is in His victory.*

May the God of hope fill you with all joy and peace as you trust in Him, so that you may overflow with hope by the power of the Holy Spirit. (Romans 15:13 NIV)

CONCLUDING PRINCIPLE:

> *You cannot understand*
> *how great the rewards*
> *will be if you obey Jesus.*

APPENDIXES

APPENDIX A

SUMMARY PAGE OF KEY PRINCIPLES

CHAPTER 1 — *You must want to change in order to change.*

CHAPTER 2 — *Life is unfair. So what?*

CHAPTER 3 — *Finish the race to win the prize.*

CHAPTER 4 — *The foundation for true success is being in a right relationship with God through faith in Jesus Christ.*

CHAPTER 5 — *Without daily reading of the Instruction Book, you can't have true wisdom.*

CHAPTER 6 — *Praising God puts the right perspective on your problems.*

CHAPTER 7 — *You cannot be forgiven until you forgive.*

CHAPTER 8 — *Blaming others delays your progress; taking responsibility hastens it.*

CHAPTER 9 — *If you don't know where you are, you can't get there from here.*

THIS IS FOR YOU

L et me help you by listing a few questions. These questions are for you; no one else will see your answers unless you want them to. Pray about each answer and answer as unto the Lord. If you want to get on top, let's deal with the facts.

Are you a Christian as defined by the Bible?

Yes ____ No ____

What was the approximate date or year you asked Jesus Christ to come into your heart?

Date: ____/____/____

How did you become a Christian?

_____

_____

_____

_____

_____

How would you describe your relationship with God?

_____

_____

_____

_____

_____

_____

_____

Would your husband or wife agree?

Yes ____ No ____

Would God agree?

Yes ____ No ____

If you are married, how would you describe your relationship with your husband or wife?

_____

_____

_____

_____

_____

_____

Would your spouse agree?

Yes ____ No ____

How often do you spend quality time sharing your heart with your spouse?

_____

_____

_____

_____

_____

_____

_____

What is the number one thing you need to do to have a godly marriage?

_____

_____

_____

_____

_____

_____

Would you and your spouse agree on that?

Yes ____ No ____

When are you going to start?

Date ___/___/___

Write out in as few words as reasonable what you think the number one problem is. You don't have to go into great detail (use other paper if needed).

_____

_____

_____

_____

_____

_____

_____

_____

_____

_____

_____

_____

Do you know where you are financially?

Yes ____ No ____

If you don't, are you ready to find out?

Yes ____ No ____

Has anyone given you advice about this problem (e.g., accountant, lawyer, pastor, or consultant)?

Yes ____ No ____

Who? _____

_____

_____

What did they advise you to do?

_____

_____

_____

_____

_____

_____

Do you think it was good advice?

Yes ___ No ___

Did you do what they suggested?

Yes ___ No ___

Why or why not?

_____

_____

_____

_____

_____

_____

What were the results?

_____

_____

_____

_____

_____

_____

Have you tried anything else?

Yes ___ No ___

Why or why not?

_____

_____

_____

_____

_____

_____

Will you keep trying?

Yes ___ No ___

Have you discussed the problem in detail with your husband or wife?

Yes ___ No ___

Why or why not?

_____

_____

_____

_____

_____

_____

Is the answer above based on God's Word?

Yes _____ No _____

What did your mate say?

_____

_____

_____

_____

_____

_____

Did it help?

Yes _____ No _____

Did you take your mate's advice?

Yes _____ No _____

Why or why not?

_____

_____

_____

_____

_____

Have you had similar problems before?

Yes ____ No ____

What was the solution before?

_____

_____

_____

_____

_____

_____

Will elements of that same solution work again?

Yes ____ No ____

How much time have you spent in prayer about this problem?

_____ hours _____ minutes per day.

This is the confidence which we have before Him, that, if we ask anything according to His will, He hears us. And if we know that He hears us in whatever we ask, we know that we have the requests which we have asked of Him.
                                        1 John 5:14–15

Do you have a prayer partner to pray with you about this problem on a regular basis?

Yes ____ No ____

If not, will you ask God to give you one?

Yes ___ No ___

And if one can overpower him who is alone, two can resist him. A cord of three strands is not quickly torn apart.
                                        Ecclesiastes 4:12

What godly person are you accountable to?

_____

Iron sharpens iron, so one man sharpens another.
                                        Proverbs 27:17

If you do not have a godly person of the same sex to be accountable to, would you like to have one?

Yes ___ No ___

If yes, will you ask God to give you one?

Yes ___ No ___

Based on the information above, what do you think your problem looks like? Sit down with your spouse or a trusted friend and discuss the whole thing to see if you can work through the part you can solve. And ask God to do the part only He can solve. Don't get the two mixed up. You do what you can do.

Now is not the time to play games with anyone, particularly God.

DISCOVERING WHERE
YOU ARE FINANCIALLY

EXAMPLE: This Is What I Owe

Description	Amount Due Now	Amount Due Long Term
Supply House	1,800	
Utilities	320	
IRS	2,200	
Office Supply	167	
Truck Repair	503	
Bank Note	4,124	12,000
Savings & Loan	900	124,500
Total	*10,014*	*136,500*

NOW YOU DO IT. LIST ALL THAT YOU OWE.

Description	Amount Due Now	Amount Due Long Term

Description of Things I Have Control Over and Can Sell or Use to Pay Debt	Net Value I Can Use Now to Pay Bills	Net Realistic Value I Can Sell It For in the Near Future
Cash in Bank	300	
Money John M. Owes Me That Is Not in Dispute	2,250	
33% of the Cost of Inventory		1,200
Delivery Truck (Present Loan Value Less 10%)	3,000	
Ford Car (Present Loan Value Less 10%)	3,200	
Warehouse (Appraised Value Less 10%) Rent Until It Sells	900	90,000
Total	9,650	91,200

This Is The Way It Looks		
	Now	Long Term
This is the amount I owe	10,014	136,500
These are assets I have to pay with	9,650	91,200
Net difference	(364)	(45,300)

Description of Things I Have Control Over and Can Sell or Use to Pay Debt	Net Value I Can Use Now to Pay Bills	Net Realistic Value I Can Sell It For in the Near Future

This Is The Way It Looks		
	Now	**Long Term**
This is the amount I owe		
These are assets I have to pay with		
Net difference		

Don't make a big deal of the whole thing. Sit down and get all the facts together. Don't worry about posting debits or credits. That's for bookkeepers and accountants. You just need the facts to know if you have a major problem or a small irritation. And you must know now, not next week or next month.

Get some help if you need to. Whatever reasons you are using for not getting this together can be no more. Now is the time. Think about it. It won't be any worse because you put it on paper.

YOUR PERSONAL GOALS

This is your worksheet. To make the best use of it, ask yourself what your condition is now and what you want it to be in six months, one year, and two years. By writing it down, you and your husband or wife can clearly define your short-term goals. Feel free to add or change any lines or items you want to. I would not recommend you plan beyond two years until you have worked with it for a while. You can change the plan as often as you need to do so. When you have completed this goals worksheet, ask yourself, What must I do to obtain these goals? That will be your action plan. I have filled out a sample so you can see how it looks. Use the blank form on the next page for your purposes.

Description	Now	Within 6 Months	Within 1 Year	Within 2 Years
Gross Annual Income	0	36,000	36,000	42,000
Minimum Income Needed	21,000	21,000	22,000	22,000
Cash on Hand	0	1,000	2,000	5,000
Major Purchases	None	None	None	Car
Education (tuition)	0	0	0	1,000
Retirement Goal	0	0	5,000	10,000
Debt Freedom				50% Debt Free
Net Worth	0	0	7,000	15,000

Description	Now	Within 6 Months	Within 1 Year	Within 2 Years

TYPES OF BANKRUPTCY

The decision to file for bankruptcy is very difficult to deal with, but I will give a brief overview of the types of bankruptcy that may be available to you. To give any more information than this would not help you but hurt you.

When a decision is being made about bankruptcy, you must have good, sound, biblically based advice to assist you in making the right decision. Some people you might ask to pray through this with you would be your spouse, your pastor, the spiritual leaders of your church, and other mature Christians.

Remember Psalm 1:1: "How blessed is the man who does not walk in the counsel of the wicked, nor stand in the path of sinners, nor sit in the seat of scoffers!" Get all of your counsel about filing bankruptcy from godly men and women.

Let me caution you: If anyone says that all you have to do to end your problems is file bankruptcy, don't believe it. As pointed out earlier in this book, there is no easy way out when you are in serious financial trouble. And the easiest way is not necessarily the most godly way, so consult other Christians for accountability and counsel.

You should also seek an honest Christian attorney. However, if I had to choose between an incompetent Christian attorney and a competent non-Christian attorney, I would choose the non-Christian.

There are four different types of bankruptcy, each with a different purpose. They are chapters 7, 11, 12, and 13.

A CHAPTER 7 BANKRUPTCY

A chapter 7 bankruptcy is the type most frequently used. It can be used by individuals or a business, and it provides for the complete liquidation of all the non-exempt property owned on the date you filed.

A court-appointed trustee collects all your assets and sells them over a period of time, and the trustee pays the creditors. Who is paid and how much depends on many factors and should be discussed with your attorney.

Many complex problems enter into deciding to file a chapter 7. If the possibility of keeping the business operating and paying back creditors is out of the question, then a chapter 7 may be an option. As with all bankruptcy decisions, you should talk to a good attorney.

A CHAPTER 11 BANKRUPTCY

A chapter 11 bankruptcy is often used when there is a possibility that the business can continue to operate. What this means is that nothing is liquidated. You keep the company and operate it while you pay off your creditors. Your plan to operate the company must be approved by the court and the creditors.

I caution you: Operating a company while in chapter 11 is extremely difficult, and only a few can cope with all of the requirements imposed by the courts. Very few companies emerge from a chapter 11. The problems that caused you to get into financial difficulty in the first place are not likely to go away.

Another reason to be sure you are up to a chapter 11 is the high cost of attorneys. This type of bankruptcy is normally used by businesses.·

A CHAPTER 12 BANKRUPTCY

A chapter 12 bankruptcy is specifically for family farmers who have too much debt to qualify for a chapter 13.

You are likely to be eligible for relief if more than 50 percent of your income and 80 percent of your debts are from farming. You also must have total debts. under $1.5 million. You must be able to show the court that you have the ability to make payments according to a court-approved plan. Effective October 1, 1998, this chapter will be repealed.

A CHAPTER 13 BANKRUPTCY

A chapter 13 bankruptcy is designed for "wage earners" or small business owners. You may keep all of your assets while the repayment plan is in effect.

The sale of assets is usually not required. If you are in business, you can continue to operate the business.

This chapter requires repayment of your debts from your income over a period of three to five years. The court has the power to reduce the amount to be paid back, except in the case of secured debts and certain other debts, such as child support and certain taxes.

Again, let me caution you about filing bankruptcy in order to "walk away." This is a serious decision that has long-term consequences. I have heard hundreds of people say they wish they had never filed for bankruptcy. The spiritual and emotional strain was greater with bankruptcy than with talking with all the creditors and working with them. Carefully examine all other options before you take this step.

Remember, all your creditors want is the money you owe them.

Let me encourage you to read as much as possible on bankruptcy before you go to an attorney. One good recent book I read on the subject of bankruptcy was *Surviving Financial Crisis* by Richard L. Strohm, a lawyer from Arizona. It is published by Law guides. The book will give you some detailed insight into what you will be facing if you file for bankruptcy.